Naturalistic, Classroom-based Reading Assessment

A Problem Solving Approach

George J. Cavuto, Ph.D.

KENDALL/HUNT PUBLISHING COMPANY
4050 Westmark Drive   Dubuque, Iowa 52002

CONTENTS

# ABOUT THE AUTHOR

Dr. George J. Cavuto is enjoying his thirty-fifth year as an educator. Dr. Cavuto has extensive experience working with students at ALL levels (from preschool through graduate school). After spending sixteen years in the public school arena, first as an English teacher and later as a Reading Specialist, Dr. Cavuto joined the Dowling College School of Education Faculty (Oakdale, NY). Dr. Cavuto presently holds the position of Professor of Literacy Education at Dowling College. He was Chairperson of the Department of Literacy Education for twelve years and Academic Chair of the School of Education for four years. Dr. Cavuto has taught graduate level courses in Literacy Acquisition, Literacy Assessment, Language Acquisition and Disorders, and Literacy Research. Dr. Cavuto has conducted numerous Professional Development Seminars and Workshops for classroom teachers, reading specialists, special educators, school administrators, and parents. His engaging presentation style, extensive knowledge base, and unique ability to "bridge" theory into practice, has made him a much sought after speaker.

Dr. Cavuto is also the owner/director of a private Literacy Research/Instruction Center, The Reading and Learning Center of Long Island Inc. (West Islip, NY), which he established in 1973. Over the past three decades, he has assessed and instructed (and/or supervised the instruction of) literally thousands of students with reading and writing difficulties. The Simple Reading Assessment Model (S-RAM) is used by Dr. Cavuto to share assessment information with the parents of his Reading and Learning Center clients. Parents have commented that its "specificity" and "logic" make it an extremely valuable assessment/information-sharing tool. It also "demystifies" reading assessment and, perhaps most importantly, INFORMS instruction. The S-RAM is being used by teachers throughout the United States as a simple, yet effective, way to engage in classroom-based, naturalistic reading/language assessment. In order to use the S-RAM effectively, teachers MUST develop, in Dr. Cavuto's terms, "knowing eyes" and "knowing ears" as they observe students engaging in authentic literacy events/activities in their classrooms.

Over the past twenty years, Dr. Cavuto has developed a program specifically designed to help "struggling readers" overcome their difficulties; his program is called, *A Process Approach to Reading (PAR)*. The major objective of this program is to bring students with reading challenges up to the level of their peers . . . up to PAR. The underlying philosophy of the *PAR PROGRAM*, as well as reading strategies consistent with the program, are discussed in this text, and extensively elaborated upon in its "companion text," *From Naturalistic, Classroom-based Reading Assessment to Informed, Balanced Instruction* (Cavuto & Schlichting, 2004), also published by Kendall/Hunt Publishing Company.

PREFACE

And so to completely analyze what we do when we read
would almost be the acme of a psychologist's
achievements, for it would be to describe very many
of the most intricate workings of the human mind. . . .

—*Edmund Burke Huey*

Reading is a problem-solving, hypothesis-testing activity. As the reader attempts to reconstruct the author's intended meaning, he/she utilizes cognitive, linguistic and perceptual resources. Some children (i.e., early/natural readers) acquire reading skills/strategies at a very young age with little apparent difficulty; other children struggle all of their school lives (and indeed, oftentimes well into adulthood) because of an inability to read. In many cases, these individuals' lives are marginalized. Clearly, there are no panaceas for remediating reading difficulties; however, the first step in "fixing" any problem is to properly "identify/assess" the problem and to establish causation if possible.

The thesis of this text is that reading assessment is a problem-solving activity that is best conducted over time as children engage in authentic literacy activities. The knowledge/conceptual base of the "observer" is of quintessential importance. The point is made throughout this text that teachers must develop the "knowing eye" and the "knowing ear" as they informally and formally assess their students' reading strategies. It is very difficult, if not impossible, for a teacher to make an accurate assessment of a student's reading skills/strategies without an in-depth understanding of the reading process. Simply stated, teachers MUST know how the reading process works if they are to correctly assess IF? WHEN?, AND WHY? the process is breaking down.

Reading, like any complex process, does not easily lend itself to "factor analysis." Indeed, attempts to break reading down into lists of discrete teaching/learning objectives to be mastered is bound to lack fruition; the "whole" is often greater than the "sum of its parts." This point notwithstanding, "knowledgeable/expert" observers of reading behavior most certainly attend to certain broad aspects of the process in order to arrive at a "tentative assessment" (to be confirmed or rejected by further observation). These broad aspects of the reading/language process are represented on the Simple Reading Assessment

Model (S-RAM) developed by this author. Included in this assessment model are Affective Domain, Decoding Accuracy, Decoding Automaticity, Reading Comprehension, Listening Comprehension, World Knowledge (Schemata), Receptive Vocabulary, and Attention/Concentration Span.

This text helps teachers become more knowledgeable re: each of these aspects of the reading/language process. Teachers are encouraged to place a plus (+) or a minus (–) in EACH part of the model for EACH of the students in their classes (i.e., a Simple Reading Assessment Model should be kept for each student in the class) based on the teacher's daily observations of the student's behavior/performance as he/she engages in authentic literacy activities. Further, teachers are taught/encouraged to establish *causation* for breakdowns in reading comprehension and listening comprehension. Causation (both primary and secondary) is illustrated on the S-RAM with *arrows* going from one aspect of the process (e.g., decoding accuracy) to another (e.g., reading comprehension).

This author firmly believes that reading assessment is important ONLY to the degree that it informs instruction. However, the main thrust of this text is naturalistic, classroom-based reading assessment. Reading instructional strategies are mentioned in this text; however, they are by no means given extensive attention. There are many excellent texts available to teachers to help them facilitate students' development in each of the areas specified on the Simple Reading Assessment Model. The author strongly recommends that teachers avail themselves of these fine resources.

Students who experience reading difficulties are usually well aware of the fact that their reading skills/strategies are lacking; however, they oftentimes perceive this deficit in a rather "general" sense . . . "I'm not a good reader. I hate to read!" My experience has been that by showing these students a Simple Reading Assessment Model (S-RAM) with areas of STRENGTH as well as areas of WEAKNESS indicated, the student gains ownership of his/her own literacy. Instead of a vaguely defined deficit, the student is able to very specifically see the areas in which he/she is strong, the areas in which he/she is weak, and then, most importantly, an instructional plan can be developed, both by the teacher *and* the student, to utilize strengths to remediate weaknesses. This is a very liberating experience for the student; it is equally liberating for the teacher. Instead of "blaming the victim," the teacher becomes the student's "partner" in helping him/her to actualize his/her optimum literacy potential.

To date, the Simple Reading Assessment Model (S-RAM) has been introduced to, and is being used by, literally thousands of classroom teachers, literacy specialists, special education teachers, school administrators, and graduate students pursuing advanced degrees in Literacy Education. Indeed, their positive comments regarding the effectiveness of this model have been the catalyst for this text. I both acknowledge and appreciate the feedback received from the aforementioned groups of educators over the past many years. A very special thank you is due the full-time and adjunct faculty members of the Literacy Education Department, as well as the graduate students, at Dowling College; their acceptance of, commitment to, and ongoing feedback re: this model have allowed it to *evolve* to its present stage.

In a speech about literacy assessment, Roger Farr stated, ". . . I have a dream that assessment will be put to use honoring what children can do rather than destroying them for what they can't do." (Farr, 1996, p. 424). The Simple Reading Assessment Model (S-RAM) allows both teachers and students to identify areas of literacy strength as well as weakness. Accurate assessment, based upon ongoing, *knowledgeable* observation, is (in this author's opinion) the best way for Farr's dream to become a reality.

I encourage all educators to strive to develop an in-depth understanding of the reading/language process. I hope that this text serves to help you to accomplish this very important goal. It is your knowledge and understanding of the process that will allow you to engage in accurate, authentic, naturalistic assessment. Assess well, teach well, change lives!

GJC

REFERENCES

Farr, R. (1996). I have a dream about assessment. *The Reading Teacher*, 49, 424.

CHAPTER 1

Reading Theory—The Critical Importance of the Conceptual Framework Underlying Reading Assessment

It appears that naturalistic, classroom-based, "ongoing" assessment of students' reading skills/strategies has finally come of age! The advantages of evaluating students' strengths/weaknesses as they engage in authentic literacy activities have been clearly articulated (Valencia, Hiebert, and Afferblach, 1994). The negatives associated with "standardized testing" (sometimes referred to as "one moment in time" testing) have long been recognized (Johnston, 1984). However, it is critically important to recognize that there is a prerequisite to being a skilled "reading kidwatcher"—the observer *must have a clear, in-depth understanding of the reading process*. Without this understanding, the observer is in the rather tenuous position of having to trust his/her "instincts" or "common-sense" judgements. E.D. Hirsch, in his text entitled *Cultural Literacy* (Hirsch, 1988), gives an excellent illustration of observing without the benefit of an informed, conceptual base: If two people are playing chess, and right in the middle of the game someone accidentally knocks off all of the pieces a novice chess player (or someone who doesn't play chess at all), who had observed the board prior to the disruption would have much difficulty replacing the pieces in their respective positions; however, a master chess player would be remarkably accurate in replacing each piece to its proper position before the disruption. Hence, the critical importance of observing with "the knowing eye," (Cavuto,1992) whether the task being observed is reading, chess, or any other human activity.

If we've learned anything at all about literacy learning over the past two decades, we've clearly come to the realization that oftentimes a teacher's "common-sense" or "instinctual" response to students' literacy behaviors may not be valid (Hoffman, 1979). One of the major premises underlying much of the content presented in this text is that in order to be competent "kidwatchers" of children's reading behaviors, teachers must have an in-depth understanding of the reading process (i.e., conceptual base); this conceptual base then becomes the backdrop against which teaching decisions (i.e., assessment and instructional) are made. This chapter will focus on four aspects of reading theory which *must be understood* by every teacher who is responsible for both assessing and facilitating children's acquisition of reading skills/strategies.

Let's begin by defining our terms: *Visual information* is the print on the page (in most cases letters and words; in some cases other kinds of symbols, diagrams, maps, graphs, etc.); this information is also referred to as *textual information.* *Nonvisual information* is the reader's sum total background knowledge (Smith, 1994). The reader's background knowledge is also referred to as *schemata* (Anderson, 1984). The principle is a simple one: The more nonvisual information the reader brings to the page, the less he/she has to rely on the visual information; conversely, the less nonvisual information the reader has to bring to the page, the more he/she has to rely on the visual information (Smith, 1994, pp. 7–13).

> **Reading Principle #1:**
> Any reader encountering any text will experience a reciprocal relationship between *visual information* and *nonvisual information* (Smith, 1994).

APPLICATION OF READING PRINCIPLE #1

If a reader is having difficulty understanding text, it may be because he/she lacks sufficient *schema* (i.e., topic specific background knowledge) to bring to the reading task. An easy way to test this hypothesis is to ask the child about several of the text's key concepts. If the child doesn't know the concepts, it is quite possible that comprehension is breaking down because he/she is engaging in *bottom-up processing* (i.e., over-utilizing the visual information and under-utilizing the nonvisual information due to a lack of appropriate schema). If you have determined that the child does have adequate and appropriate schema to bring to the reading task and is still not comprehending, it may be due to his/her inability to *instantiate* this schema (i.e., the child knows a lot about the topic but is not bringing this information to the page as he/she attempts to construct meaning from the text (Anderson and Pearson, 1984). There may, in fact, be other reasons for the reader's comprehension difficulty that have nothing to do with insufficient nonvisual information; these reasons (i.e., causal factors) will be discussed in subsequent chapters of this text.

Reading Principle #1 is a critically important one. It is not new—it is simply worth repeating and stressing! When teachers are encouraged (e.g., by a Basal Reader Teacher's Guide) to ask children the meaning of key vocabulary words before reading a story, they are, in effect, assessing the children's individual and collective schemas re: the story to be read. When a social studies teacher asks the class to brainstorm all that they know about the War of 1812 before they begin to read about it in their textbook, he/she is both *assessing* (i.e., evaluating) and *accessing* (bringing it to the conscious, working part of memory) the readers' nonvisual information.

If the students, in either of the situations described above, have limited schema to bring to the text (either individually or collectively), the teacher should realize that it will be that much more difficult for the students to comprehend the text because they will be forced to engage in bottom-up processing (i.e., overutilizing visual information). Teachers who understand this principle take steps to fill in any voids in background knowledge before the students are asked to read the textbook independently. By so doing, students will be better able to engage in *top-down processing* (i.e., constructing text meaning by the use of nonvisual information).

As F. Smith has suggested, we haven't been able to answer the question, "What is the best way to teach reading?" because it is the wrong question (Smith, 1994). We have learned from the linguists (Chomsky, 1957) that all written languages contain *graphophonic cues* (letter/sound correspondences), *syntactic cues* (word order relationships), and *semantic cues* (meaning). Indeed, these are often referred to as *linguistic universals* because they are common to all languages. Researchers (Goodman, 1967; Smith, 1994) have suggested that developing proficiency in reading involves learning how to flexibly use all three language cueing systems as one attempts to process meaningful discourse.

English IS a phonetic language: indeed, there are 42 distinct *phonemes* (sounds) in English. Unfortunately, the English alphabet only has 26 *graphemes* (letters) to represent these sounds; therefore, there are two types of words in English: *phonetically consistent* (i.e., "sound-outable") words, and *phonetically inconsistent* ("not sound-outable") words.

Reading Principle #2: Meaningful textual discourse has *three language cueing systems* embedded in it. Competent readers *flexibly* use all three of these systems as they attempt to accurately reconstruct the writer's intended message.

APPLICATION OF READING PRINCIPLE #2

If children are given meaningful text to read, the three language cueing systems embedded in the text will be available for them to use in their attempt to accurately reconstruct the author's intended meaning. The teacher's task is to teach the children how to flexibly/effectively use cue system strategies. However, if children are given nonmeaningful text (e.g., nonsense words, words in isolation), they are limited to using graphophonic cues only—making the reading that much more difficult (and sometimes, in the case of phonetically inconsistent words, impossible!)

As children attempt to process meaningful text and they have difficulty decoding/identifying a word, they should be encouraged to utilize all three language cueing systems available to them. After they make a hypothesis (i.e., attempt the word), they should cross-check this hypothesis by asking the following questions: Does it make sense? (i.e., using *semantic/meaning* cues to cross check); Does it sound like an acceptable English language structure? (i.e., using *syntactic/word order/grammar* cues to cross-check); Does it look right? (i.e., using *graphophonic/symbol-sound* cues to cross-check). If their answer to any of these three questions is "No," they should rehypothesize.

For example, if a child reads, "The little boy and his friend came home from school. They opened the door and went into the *horse.* They had a snack in the kitchen and then went upstairs to play." The miscue "horse" for "house" clearly indicates that the reader is attending reasonably well to *graphophonic cues* (i.e., the miscue has a clear graphophonic resemblance to the text word); it also indicates that the reader is attending reasonably well to *syntactic cues* (both "horse" and "house" are nouns); however, he/she is clearly not attending to the author's intended meaning (this miscue significantly distorts the author's intended meaning). This type of miscue, particularly if it is made often, is a clear indication to the reading kidwatcher with the "knowing eye" that the child is not reading for meaning and hasn't learned how to *self-monitor* (i.e., ongoing self-evaluation of his/her comprehension or lack thereof). These are very important assessments and should be followed-up with appropriate instruction (i.e., strategy lessons) in using semantic cues and self-monitoring for meaning.

If a child is reading the sentence, "The big red dog came to live with us. He was a huge dog. He was the largest dog that I had ever seen," and he/she miscued on the word "largest" reading it "biggest," the knowing reading kidwatcher realizes that this is a semantically acceptable miscue (it does not distort the author's intended meaning) and leaves the miscue uncorrected. Indeed, the knowing kidwatcher understands that this kind of miscue is a sign of reader strength (it shows that he/she is predicting and constructing meaning) rather than reader weakness. The knowing kidwatcher also knows how to respond to other children in the group who may be surprised that the miscue is left uncorrected.

Informed response to a student's oral reading miscues is no simple matter. In fact, it requires an in-depth understanding of the reading process (reading theory), the ability to distinguish between facilitative feedback and feedback that may inhibit the reader, and the ability to provide feedback which will enable the reader to develop more mature reading strategies (Zutell, 1977). To be a knowing reading kidwatcher without a firm grounding in the body of research dealing with oral reading miscues and miscue analysis would appear to be virtually impossible. As K. Goodman points out, a student's oral reading miscues are not things to be eradicated; rather, they are valuable in that they provide the listener with a "window on the reader's processes" (Goodman, 1969). This "window" is only available, however, to those who are well versed in classroom applications of this naturalistic assessment technique. (Note: See chapter 3 for a more detailed explanation of oral reading miscues and miscue analysis.)

Reading Principle #3: Readers' *oral reading miscues* (i.e., deviations from text) are particularly illuminating of the *language cueing systems* they are using (or not using) as they attempt to process printed information (Goodman, 1969).

Reading Principle #4:
The more attention the reader has to give to the task of *word identification/decoding*, the less attention he/she will have available for *comprehension*.

As readers (of any age) attempt to process meaningful text, they are constantly attempting to do two things simultaneously: decode the words (break the orthographic code) and comprehend the text (LaBerge and Samuels, 1974). If the reader has significant difficulty breaking the code (i.e., cannot identify/decode many words in the text), it will be very difficult, if not impossible, for him/her to accurately reconstruct the author's intended meaning. If the reader can identify/decode the words on the page, however, he/she is not able to engage in *automatic word identification/decoding* (i.e., one second or less identification/decoding), on the majority of words in the text, he/she will most likely have difficulty comprehending the text; this difficulty will be a direct consequence of a *trade off of attention* (i.e., he/she is giving so much attention/energy to the word identification/decoding task that there is simply not enough attention/energy remaining to be directed to the important task of comprehending the text).

APPLICATION OF READING PRINCIPLE #4

While observing a student interact with text, if it appears that he/she is taking an inordinate amount of time to read the text, it may be the result of poor word identification/decoding accuracy or lack of word identification automaticity. Word identification that is not automatic is referred to as *mediated word identification* (Smith, 1994). A student who engages in much mediated word identification is predisposed to being both a slow reader (because of the lack of automaticity) and a poor comprehender (because of the trade off of attention).

If the knowing reading kidwatcher observes a child *overmediating* (i.e., engaging in a significant amount of non-automatic word identification/decoding) with a grade level text, he/she knows that this student will need to do extensive recreational reading at independent levels in order to increase automaticity. If the knowing reading kidwatcher notices that a child is not comprehending the text because he/she is experiencing considerable difficulty word identifying/decoding the words in the text, then the instructional intervention may involve:

1. "buddying the child up" with a more proficient word identifier/decoder in the class;

2. putting the book on tape and allowing the child to listen to the tape as he/she follows along in the book (note: the tape must be slow enough for the student to follow along in the text);

3. providing the child with strategy lessons in meaningful contexts where he/she is taught how to flexibly use all three language cueing systems to decode words that are not immediately recognizeable/decodable.

It would be naive to suggest that by simply learning the aforementioned reading principles, classroom teachers would become expert in naturalistic, classroom-based assessment of students' reading; however, it is reasonable to suggest that by learning, and learning well, the principles outlined above, classroom teachers will most certainly hone their assessment skills. Indeed, once they have mastered these principles and their applications, they will be well on their way to developing more "knowing eyes and ears" (Cavuto, 1992). They will also be better prepared to discuss, in detail, their students' reading strengths/weaknesses with colleagues, administrators, teachers, and the students themselves. Most importantly, as teachers increase their "kidwatching skills," they will use these skills to inform their instruction; let us not forget, assessment is meaningless if it doesn't inform instruction.

FOLLOW-UP EXERCISES

Directions: Read the following scenarios and answer the questions that follow.

1. Joseph is a ninth-grade student. His content area teachers have observed significant gaps in his background knowledge (schemata).

    Question #1: Is Joseph most likely going to be a top-down processor of content area text or a bottom-up processor of content area text? Explain your answer.

    Question #2: Is Joseph going to have satisfactory reading comprehension or unsatisfactory reading comprehension of his content area textbooks? Explain your answer.

    Question #3: Is Joseph going to be able to effectively use the semantic cueing system as he reads? Explain your answer.

2. Brenda is a second-grade student. Her classroom teacher has observed the following during episodes of oral reading: When Brenda is not able to immediately identify/decode a word, her first strategy is to skip the word and read to the end of the sentence. If that doesn't work, Brenda attempts to sound out the word. When Brenda is satisfied with her "guess" for that word, she re-reads the entire sentence, smiling and nodding her head after completing the sentence. This process is habitual; it is clearly the way that Brenda deals with printed information.

    Question #1: Does Brenda appear to be flexibly using all three cueing systems as she reads? Explain your answer.

    Question #2: Does Brenda appear to be self-monitoring as she reads? Explain your answer.

    Question #3: Based upon the limited information provided, would you predict that Brenda has satisfactory reading comprehension or unsatisfactory reading comprehension? Explain your answer.

3. Joey, a five-year-old child, has been read to by his parents on a regular basis since he was a year old. Jenny, Joey's neighbor and friend, who is also five years old, is very rarely read to by her parents. They are about to enter the first grade.

    Question #1: Does Joey have a better chance of becoming a proficient reader (i.e., reading comprehender) than Jenny? Explain your answer.

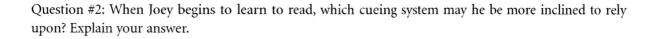

Question #2: When Joey begins to learn to read, which cueing system may he be more inclined to rely upon? Explain your answer.

Question #3: When Jenny begins to learn to read, which cueing system may she be more inclined to rely upon? Explain your answer.

4. Mercedes, a sixth-grade student, makes many oral reading miscues when she is asked to read aloud in class. Her teacher has observed the following:

   • her miscues tend to resemble the text word in terms of letter (grapheme) sound (phoneme) relationships;

   • her miscues tend to retain the author's intended meaning;

   • she almost always self-corrects miscues that significantly distort the author's intended meaning.

Question #1: Based upon this limited information, do you think that Mercedes has satisfactory reading comprehension or poor reading comprehension? Explain your answer.

Question #2: Based upon this limited information, do you think that Mercedes is doing more "top-down processing" or more "bottom-up processing"? Explain your answer.

Question #3: Is Mercedes a "risk-taker" as she processes text? Explain your answer.

References

Anderson, Richard. C., & Pearson, P. David. (1984). "A Schema-Theoretic View of Basic Processes in Reading Comprehension." In P. David Pearson, Rebecca Barr, Michael L. Kamil, & Peter Mosenthal (Eds.), *Handbook of Reading Research* (pp. 255–291). New York: Longman.

Cavuto, George. (1992, October/November). "Kidwatching: Helping Teachers Develop the Knowing Eye." *Reading Today,* p. 28.

Chomsky, N. (1957). *Syntactic Structures.* The Hague: Mouton, 1957.

Goodman, K.S. (1967). "Reading: A Psycholinguistic Guessing Game." *Journal of the Reading Specialist,* 6, 126–135.

Goodman, K.S. (1969). "Analysis of Reading Miscues: Applied Psycholinguistics." *Reading Research Quarterly,* 5, 9–30.

Hirsch, E.D., Jr. (1987). *Cultural Literacy.* Boston: Houghton-Mifflin Co.

Hoffman, James V. (1979). "On Providing Feedback to Reading Miscues." *Reading World,* 18, 342–349.

Johnston, Peter H. (1992). "Evaluation Mythology: A Critical Look at Tests and Testing." In *Constructive Evaluation of Literate Activity* (pp. 337–338). New York: Longman

LaBerge, D., & Samuels, S.J. (1974). "Toward a Theory of Automatic Information Processing in Reading." *Cognitive Psychology,* 6, 293–323.

Smith, Frank. (1994). *Understanding Reading* (5th ed.) Hillsdale, NJ: Lawrence Erlbaum Assoc., Inc.

Valencia, Sheila W., Hiebert, Elfrieda H., & Afflerbach, Peter P. (Eds.). (1994) *Authentic Reading Assessment: Practices and Possibilities.* Newark, DE: International Reading Association.

Zutell, Jerome B. (1977). "Teacher Informed Response to Reader Miscue." *Theory into Practice,* 16, 384–390.

CHAPTER 2

Word Identification/Decoding

Key Words/Terms

word identification, decoding, word identification/decoding accuracy, immediate/automatic word identification/decoding, mediated word identification/decoding, sight words, basic sight word storehouse, trade off of attention principle, meaning-retaining miscues, meaning-distorting miscues

Identifying words in text, also referred to as *word identification* or *decoding*, involves breaking the written code of language. Spoken language is a code, a culturally agreed upon means of communication. When spoken words are *encoded* (i.e., put into written form), it becomes the reader's task to break the written code in an attempt to accurately reconstruct the author's intended meaning—hence the term *decoding*.

Clearly, the ultimate goal of reading is to process meaning; however, it becomes very difficult, if not impossible, to get at the author's intended meaning without being able to break the written code. Two simple examples should illustrate this point:

1. A message is sent to you in Morse Code—it is a very simple message indeed; however, if you don't know how to decode the series of dots and dashes, there is no way that you can get at the meaning of the message.

2. Your colleague hands you a book intended for blind individuals; the book is written in Braille (i.e., raised dots in different configurations). If you do not know Braille, you will be unable to break the code; therefore, it will be impossible to decipher the author's intended message.

Word identification/decoding is NOT what reading is all about; reading is about a search for meaning. However, as you can see from the previous examples, *breaking the code* is a critical aspect of any meaning getting process.

Immediate vs. Mediated Word Identification/Decoding

When a reader attempts to identify/decode a word in print, there are three possible outcomes:

1. the reader decodes the word incorrectly (e.g., he/she may read the word "horse" for the word "house").

2. the reader decodes the word correctly/accurately but not automatically (i.e., it takes the reader more than one second to decode the word).

3. the reader decodes the word correctly/accurately and automatically (i.e., it takes the reader less than one second to decode the word).

To review some important points from chapter 1: When a reader reads a word differently than it is printed on the page during either oral reading or silent reading, we call this a *miscue* (Goodman, 1969). [Note: Miscues will be discussed at greater length in chapter 3.] When a reader decodes a word correctly (i.e., as it is printed on the page) but not automatically (i.e., it takes more than one second to identify/decode the word), we say that the reader has engaged in *mediated word identification/decoding*. When a reader decodes a word correctly/accurately (as it's printed on the page) and automatically (it takes one second or less to identify/decode the word), we say that the reader has engaged in *immediate word identification/decoding* (Smith, 1994).

Frank Smith (Smith, 1994) makes the very interesting point that reading is "paradoxical"; from day one in school we teach children how to sound out words, hoping that they eventually stop doing this. Smith is suggesting that when we first begin to teach children to read, invariably we teach them to sound out some of the words as one means of breaking the code. As children engage in this sounding out process, they are engaging in mediated word identification/decoding. This is why most beginning readers read in a slow, laborious manner—they are mediating the words. Only after they see the words many times in many different contexts (by engaging in extensive reading of authentic texts) does their word identification/decoding become more automatic.

Words that a reader can recognize automatically are often referred to as *sight words*. The storehouse of words that a reader can recognize automatically is often referred to as the reader's *basic sight vocabulary*. The problem with this phrase is that it can cause assessment confusions. For example, if a child attempts to read the word "mother" and says ["muh . . . uh . . . thuh . . . er"] and then puts it together and says "mother," clearly he/she has decoded the word correctly/accurately;

however, he/she has engaged in mediated word identification. For this reason, this word would not be considered part of the reader's basic sight vocabulary. Here's the problem: When we think of, or use, the term vocabulary (as will be discussed in chapter 4), we are clearly referring to word meanings. Clearly, the word "mother" is part of the child's speaking and listening vocabularies; however, it would not be considered part of his/her basic sight vocabulary because it is not a word that he/she can decode automatically.

To avoid this confusion, throughout this text I will use the phrase *basic sight word storehouse* to refer to the storehouse of words that a reader can recognize automatically (in one second or less). [Note: The phrase basic sight vocabulary is more widely used in the professional literature.]

Food for Thought

Most things that we learn to do in life are learned in a mediated manner. Only with lots of practice do they become automatized.

- Children learning to add and subtract oftentimes use their fingers (mediated calculations). Only with much practice are they able to do these calculations "in their heads" without their fingers (automatic calculations).

- Children and/or adults learning to play a musical instrument often look at their fingers (mediated playing). Only with much practice are they able to have the proper "fingering" without looking (automatic playing).

- Children and/or adults learning keyboarding/typing skills are repeatedly told by their instructors not to look at their fingers! If they continue to do so, they will be continually engaging in mediated keyboarding. It is impossible to develop automatic/immediate keyboarding/typing skills if one mediates regularly.

- Children and/or adults learning to play tennis are often told by their instructors to bend their knees and get their rackets back. As the novice tennis player consciously thinks about these two techniques, he/she is playing tennis in a mediated manner; however, after playing lots of tennis, these skills will become unconscious/automatic.

Clearly, skills in any area of human endeavor, be they reading, math, typing, playing the piano or tennis, are initially performed by most learners in a mediated fashion; it is only after a significant amount of authentic practice that these skills may reach the automatic stage. There are exceptions to this rule: There are some "gifted" early readers, math students, typists, pianists, and tennis players who appear to have a degree of automaticity even as novices; clearly, these individuals are the exceptions rather than the rule.

APPLICATION

As you can see by looking at the diagram (Figure 2-1), the Word Identification/Decoding Section of the Simple Reading Assessment Model (S-RAM) is divided into two parts:

1. Word Identification/Decoding Accuracy

2. Word Identification/Decoding Automaticity

It is very important to determine the following for each student in your class:

1. Is he/she able to decode Grade Level Texts with 90 percent or better decoding/word identification accuracy? (counting meaning-retaining miscues as correct [see chapter 4]. If so, you should place a plus mark (+) in the decoding/word identification accuracy section of the S-RAM indicating that he/she has a Strength in the word identification/decoding accuracy aspect of the reading process. If not, you should place a minus sign (−) in the decoding/word identification accuracy section of the model, indicating that he/she has a Weakness in word identification/decoding accuracy.

Figure 2-1. Simple Reading Assessment Model (S-Ram).

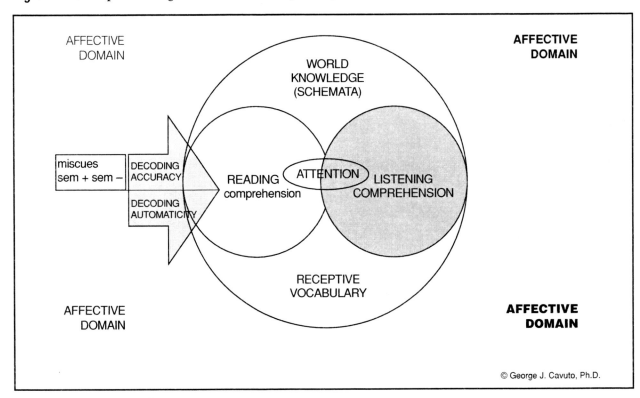

© George J. Cavuto, Ph.D.

2. Once you have determined whether or not the student is able to decode Grade Level Texts with 90 percent or better decoding/word identification accuracy, then you must determine whether or not he/she can engage in *automatic* decoding/word recognition of Grade Level Texts. If you have determined (based on the criterion level of 90 or better decoding/word recognition accuracy) that decoding accuracy/word recognition is a Weakness for this student, decoding/word recognition *automaticity* MUST also be a weakness. It would be inherently contradictory to suggest that a student has significant difficulty *correctly* decoding words in his/her Grade Level Texts; however, he/she is able to decode/identify them "automatically" (albeit *incorrectly*).

Once you have determined (by having the student read texts at incrementally lower levels than his/her Grade Level Texts) the level of text at which the student CAN decode/identify words with 90 percent or better decoding/word identification accuracy, THEN you can apply a criterion level of 70 percent or better decoding/word identification automaticity to determine whether the student is engaging primarily in *automatic decoding/word recognition* AT THIS LEVEL or *non-automatic (mediated) decoding/word recognition* AT THIS LEVEL. Hence, if the student's decoding/word recognition accuracy level is BELOW the level of the student's Grade Level Texts, even if the 70 percent criterion for decoding/word identification automaticity is met, it still has to be considered a Weakness. Conversely, if a student has better than 90 percent decoding/word recognition accuracy when reading his/her Grade Level Texts and more than 70 percent decoding/word identification automaticity when reading these same texts, then BOTH decoding /word recognition accuracy AND decoding word recognition automaticity would be considered areas of Strength for this student.

Simply stated: It is POSSIBLE for the following patterns of decoding/word identification accuracy and decoding/word identification automaticity to exist: Strength in decoding/word identification accuracy and Strength in decoding/word identification automaticity; Strength in decoding/word identification accuracy and Weakness in decoding/word identification automaticity; and Weakness in decoding/word identification accuracy and Weakness in decoding/word identification automaticity. It is IMPOSSIBLE for the following pattern to exist: Weakness in decoding/word identification accuracy, Strength in decoding/word identification automaticity.

Using the aforementioned "guidelines," if a student has a Strength in decoding/word identification automaticity, you should place a plus mark (+) in the decoding/word identification automaticity section of the S-RAM. If a student has a Weakness in decoding/word identification automaticity, you should place a minus mark (–) in this section of the model.

Suggestions for Naturalistic/Classroom-Based Assessment of Word Identification/Decoding Accuracy and Word Identification/Decoding Automaticity

- Make yourself knowledgeable re: the approximate reading levels of the texts that you have in your classroom (see chapter 9). Observe your students as they engage in both oral and silent reading of these texts. Clearly, if you are teaching second grade, and a child in your class is reading aloud from a book that is at a 2-2 (second half of second grade) reading level and he/she correctly/accurately decodes (counting meaning retaining miscues as correct) 90 percent or more of the words, then this observation would provide you with some evidence that his/her word identification/ decoding accuracy may be a strength. If you consistently observe this kind of behavior (i.e., 90 percent or better word identification/decoding accuracy of grade level text), then you should put a plus (+) sign in the Word Identification/Decoding Accuracy section of the Simple Reading Assessment Model (S-RAM), indicating that this youngster has a definite Strength in this aspect of the reading process.

- Conversely, if you are teaching fifth grade, and a child in your class is reading his/her social studies text silently and you notice that he/she appears to be struggling to identify/decode the words accurately, you can arrange to meet with that youngster in a 1-1 conference and ask the student to read a passage from the text silently; then ask him/her to read the same passage aloud. If he/she is not able to identify/decode the words with 90 percent or better accuracy (counting meaning retaining miscues as correct), then this observation would provide you with some evidence that his Word Identification/Decoding Accuracy may be a Weakness. If you consistently observe this kind of behavior (i.e., less than 90 percent word identification/ decoding accuracy of grade level text), then you should put a minus (−) sign in the Word Identification/Decoding Accuracy section of the S-RAM, indicating that this youngster has a definite Weakness in this aspect of the reading process.

- The aforementioned procedures should be followed in the same manner (with a slightly different criterion level) with respect to Word Identification/Decoding automaticity: If a student consistently reads grade level text with 70 percent or better word identification/decoding automaticity, then these observations would provide you with ample evidence that his/her Word Identification/Decoding Automaticity is a Strength. A plus sign (+) should be placed in the Word Identification/ Decoding Automaticity section of the S-RAM. Conversely, if the youngster consistently decodes grade level text with less than 70 percent Word Identification/Decoding Automaticity, a minus (−) sign should be placed in the Word Identification/Decoding Automaticity section of the S-RAM, indicating a Weakness in this aspect of the reading process.

Remember—Reading assessment is valuable only to the degree that it informs instruction! What, then, are the instructional implications that follow from the aforementioned assessment of a student's Word Identification/Decoding Accuracy and his/her Word Identification/Decoding Automaticity?

Instructional Implication #1

If the child has a weakness in Word Identification/Decoding Accuracy, the next step is for the teacher to decide WHY this student is a poor "word identifier/ decoder." An examination of the student's oral reading miscues (see chapter 3) will provide the teacher with a "window on the reader's processes" (Goodman, 1969). In other words, by noting and analyzing the student's oral reading miscues, the teacher will be able to tell which of the three language cueing systems the child is using and which one(s) he/she is not using as he/she attempts to process written discourse.

[Note: Remember, analyzing two, three or even ten miscues does not an assessment make! Like any naturalistic assessment, it is most valid to look for patterns of miscues that you observe over days, weeks, and indeed, even months. Patterns of oral reading miscues provide the listener with a "window on the reader's processing" (Goodman, 1969). More simply stated, patterns of oral reading miscues allow the listener to draw reasonable conclusions about which language cueing systems the reader is using/not using on a regular basis. This information will then be used to devise a plan for instructional intervention.]

Example #1: Jason, a second-grade student, consistently makes oral reading miscues that have very little resemblance to the text word in terms of letter/sound relationships; they are usually the same part of speech as the text word; and, they almost always rather significantly distort the author's intended meaning. This kind of ongoing observation would most probably indicate that Jason has poor knowledge of grapheme/phoneme relationships (i.e., phonics); it would also indicate that he has at least some understanding that that which he is reading has to "sound like an acceptable English Language structure" (i.e., Jason's miscues are the same part of speech as the text word); however, Jason lacks the most critical insight that a reader must have—it has to make sense! (Smith, 1994).

What kind of instructional plan should follow from the aforementioned observations of Jason's oral reading (including an analysis of his oral reading miscues)?

1. Jason is in need of direct, systematic instruction in symbol (grapheme)/sound (phoneme) relationships. More simply stated, he needs instruction in phonics. His oral reading miscues have little resemblance to the text word; this would indicate that he lacks appropriate knowledge of grapheme/phoneme relationships. There are three distinct ways of facilitating a student's use of the graphophonic cueing system during reading

(i.e., teaching phonics): letter-by-letter phonics; rule-based phonics; and letter clusters/orthographic patterns (Stahl, 1992).

2. Jason needs to be taught to self-monitor AND self-correct as he reads. Self-monitoring is defined as the reader's ongoing self-assessment of his/her state of comprehension. Clearly, Jason is not self-monitoring on a regular basis. If he were doing so, he would at least make an attempt to self-correct the oral reading miscues that significantly distort the author's intended meaning (i.e., meaning-distorting miscues). Jason must be encouraged to ask himself, "Does that make sense?" when struggling with a word that he is not immediately able to identify/decode; and after each sentence of print is processed. By doing so, Jason will begin to condition himself to search for meaning and, indeed, construct meaning as he processes text. If the answer to Jason's self-query is, "Yes, it does make sense," he should be encouraged to continue reading. If the answer is, "No, it does not make sense," Jason should be encouraged to make another attempt to identify/decode the word (using all three language cueing systems); he must attempt to formulate a hypothesis as to the decoding of the word that does make sense; and/or re-read the sentence and try to find the word that caused the sentence not to make sense. Then, Jason should be encouraged to use all three language cueing systems to re-hypothesize a word that does make sense in this particular context.

[Note: Reading is a problem-solving, hypothesis-testing activity. Readers need to be taught to constantly hypothesize, cross check for meaning, (through the flexible use of all three language cueing systems) continue on if it makes sense, reject the hypothesis and re-hypothesize if it does not make sense.]

Example #2: Linda is a student in the fourth grade. When she reads her content area textbooks (e.g., science, social studies), which are most likely written at a fifth grade level [see "Helpful Hint below re: readability of content area textbooks], her word identification/decoding accuracy is consistently above 90 percent; however, her word identification/decoding automaticity is consistently significantly less than 70 percent when she reads any of the aforementioned texts. These observations that were made over time as Linda engaged in authentic reading tasks would indicate the following: Word identification/decoding accuracy is a Strength; however, word identification/decoding automaticity is a Weakness. In short, Linda decodes well; however, she lacks automaticity in word identification/decoding. This is causing Linda to be a very slow processor of print. It takes her significantly longer than her classmates to complete any assignments that involve reading text.

What kind of instructional plan should follow from the aforementioned observations of Linda's oral reading?

1. Clearly, Linda does not need any work whatsoever in word identification/decoding accuracy. This is a Strength. She does not require work in phonics.

2. Linda does need to develop *automaticity* in word identification/decoding. Linda still has to mediate many words that, at this point in her development, should be recognized immediately/automatically (i.e., at sight). One of the best ways to develop word identification/decoding automaticity is to do extensive silent reading at independent levels with gradual, incremental increases in difficulty as each book is completed. Linda's teacher noted (through her daily, ongoing observations of Linda's reading as well as a one-to-one informal assessment [an Informal Reading Inventory] that Linda's word identification/decoding was automatic (i.e., at and above the 70 percent criterion) when she read easy second-grade-level texts from the classroom library; as soon as she attempted to move to books written at a third grade level, she began to engage in much mediated (i.e., not automatic) word identification/decoding. Thus, based upon this observation, the teacher should provide Linda with several choices of books on the second grade level to read silently at home. Clearly, these should be books that have content appropriate for her age/grade/maturity level. After Linda completes each book at home, she should be given choices of books at a slightly higher reading level (Note: incremental, not grade level, increases in difficulty). This process should be continued until such a time that Linda is able to read grade level texts, including content area texts, with 70 percent word identification/decoding automaticity.

Helpful hint: Content area textbooks (e.g., science, social studies) are typically written at least one year above the grade for which they are intended. The reason for this has to do with the fact that content area textbooks typically introduce new, fairly sophisticated vocabulary words (polysyllabic words) that represent concepts; also, the sentences in content area textbooks tend to be somewhat longer than those in narrative texts. In that most estimates of readability rely on syllable count and sentence length, it is obvious why these texts tend to be somewhat more difficult than narrative texts. It is critically important for teachers to be aware of this fact as they assess their students' reading skills/strategies.

CONCEPT REVIEW: THE TRADE OFF OF ATTENTION PRINCIPLE

As was stated in chapter 1, the more attention a reader has to give to figuring out the words (i.e., word identification/decoding), the less attention he/she has available to give to comprehending the author's intended meaning. Some researchers (LaBerge and Samuels, 1974) refer to this same concept as *cognitive capacity.* They suggest that all readers come to a page of text with a certain amount of cognitive capacity. If they utilize too much of that capacity on the process of word identification/decoding, there will be less available to devote to the primary task of reading, reconstructing the author's intended meaning.

This trade off of attention principle is very important, but all too often ignored, in assessing a student's reading. A student who has grade appropriate word identification/decoding skills but lacks automaticity in decoding/word identification is predisposed to having reading comprehension difficulties because of a trade off of attention.

FOLLOW-UP EXERCISES

Directions: Read the following scenarios and answer the questions that follow.

Scenario One: José is in the fifth grade. His teacher has made the following observations: When José reads his fifth-grade social studies and science textbooks, he makes many miscues (i.e., approximately 50–60 percent word identification/decoding accuracy); the majority of his oral reading miscues resemble the text word graphophonically, are the same part of speech as the text word, and significantly distort the author's intended meaning. José rarely, if ever, self-corrects his miscues. A majority of the words that he encounters in these texts have to be mediated.

Question #1: Is Word Identification/Decoding Accuracy a strength or weakness for José? Explain your answer.

Question #2: Is Word Identification/Decoding Automaticity a strength or weakness for José? Explain your answer.

Question #3: Is José more likely a slow reader of print or a fast reader of print? Explain your answer.

Question #4: What conclusion would you draw about José's basic sight word storehouse?

Question #5: Although the teacher does not provide us with any specific information about José's reading comprehension, do you believe that he has satisfactory (i.e., grade appropriate) reading comprehension or inadequate (i.e., below grade level) reading comprehension? Explain your answer.

Question #6: Based upon the limited information given, do you believe that José needs direct, systematic instruction in phonics? Explain your answer.

Question #7: Does José consistently engage in self-monitoring as he reads? Explain your answer.

Question #8: Does José enjoy being called upon to read aloud in class? Why? Why not?

Question #9: Based upon the limited information given, what kind of instructional plan would you devise for José in order to help him become a more proficient reader?

Scenario Two: Mark is a sixth-grade student. His teacher's classroom-based observations of his reading (over time) indicate that his ability to identify/decode words with 90 percent or better accuracy (counting meaning-retaining miscues as correct) is on approximately the seventh-grade level. His ability to identify/decode (with 70 percent or greater automaticity) is on approximately the fourth-grade level.

Question #1: When Mark reads his content area textbooks (silently or aloud), is he going to make many miscues? Explain your answer.

Question #2: When Mark reads his content area textbooks (silently or aloud), is he most likely to be a fast reader or a slow reader? Explain your answer.

Question #3: Based upon the limited information provided, do you think that Mark will have satisfactory or unsatisfactory reading comprehension following his reading of content area texts? Explain your answer.

Scenario Three: Allison is an eighth-grade student. Her English teacher has observed that Allison consistently identifies/decodes words accurately when reading grade/age appropriate text. She has also observed that Allison consistently engages in mostly immediate/automatic decoding/word identification when reading these books.

Question #1: When Allison is called upon to read aloud in her English class, does she make many oral reading miscues? Explain your answer.

Question #2: Is Allison more likely a fast reader of print or a slow reader of print? Explain your answer.

Question #3: Based upon the limited information provided, would you expect Allison to have satisfactory reading comprehension, unsatisfactory reading comprehension, or is there not enough information given to make a guess about her reading comprehension? Explain your answer.

REFERENCES

Goodman, K.S. (1969). "Analysis of Reading Miscues: Applied Psycholinguistics." *Reading Research Quarterly*, 5, 9–30.

LaBerge, D., and Samuels, S.J. (1974). "Toward a Theory of Automatic Information Processing in Reading." *Cognitive Psychology*, 6, 293–323.

Smith, Frank. (1994). *Understanding Reading* (5th ed.) Hillsdale, NJ: Lawrence Erlbaum Assoc., Inc.

Stahl, Steven A. (1992). "Saying the P Word: Nine Guidelines for Exemplary Phonics Instruction." *The Reading Teacher*, 8, 59–66.

CHAPTER 3

Oral Reading Miscues

Key Words/Terms

deviations from text, oral reading errors, oral reading miscues, miscue analysis procedure, qualitative analysis, quantitative analysis, Reading Miscue Inventory (RMI), Modified Miscue Analysis Form (MMAF), high graphophonic miscue, low graphophonic miscue, syntactically acceptable miscue, syntactically unacceptable miscue, semantically acceptable miscue, semantically unacceptable miscue, self-corrected miscue, self-monitor, formal miscue analysis, reading instructional level, product, process, mental miscue analysis (MMA), miscue patterns, perceptually parsimonious

As readers attempt to process written text, there is an interaction/transaction which takes place between the reader and the text (see chapter 1). The text has three sources of information (cues) available to the reader: graphophonic cues (letter sound relationships), syntactic cues (grammar/word order cues), and semantic cues (meaning/context cues).

As the reader attempts to accurately reconstruct the author's intended meaning, he/she uses this text-based information; however, part of this meaning construction process involves the reader using his/her background knowledge (schemata) to:

1. make predictions/hypotheses about that which is coming next in the text;

2. confirm/reject/reformulate hypotheses;

3. relate the text information to pre-existing background knowledge ("relating new to known").

Table 3-1.

Miscue Analysis									
Text Word	miscue	high gp	low gp	syn acc	syn unacc	sem acc	sem un	sc +	sc –

As the reader uses text-based information (cueing systems) and non-text based information (schema/schemata) to process the text, sometimes he/she may read a word (or perhaps an entire phrase) differently from the way in which it is printed on the page. Historically, this kind of deviation from text had been referred to as an oral reading error ; however, K. Goodman (1967) makes a convincing case that they should be called *oral reading miscues*.

K. Goodman believes that the phrase *oral reading error* is inappropriate and, indeed, misleading since it suggests that all *deviations from print* are bad and should be corrected. He makes the excellent point that as readers transact with text, invariably deviations from print will occur; these deviations are the result of the integration of text-based (i.e., language cueing systems) and non-text based (i.e., schema/schemata) information—hence the term *miscues*. K. Goodman suggests that rather than something to be "eradicated," miscues are valuable in that they provide the listener with ". . . a window on the reader's processing."

(Goodman, 1967). He believes that by qualitatively analyzing a reader's miscues by conducting a "miscue analysis," the listener/teacher will be able to determine which cueing systems the reader is utilizing effectively and which he/she (Y. Goodman and Burke, 1972) is not utilizing effectively.

An assessment instrument called the Reading Miscue Inventory allows teachers to engage in a very sophisticated, qualitative analysis of students' oral reading miscues. Numerous literacy experts/researchers/professors of literacy education have modified this instrument to make it a bit more "user friendly." The following Modified Miscue Analysis Form (Table 3-1) was developed by this author; however, the theoretical concepts underlying this form, as well as the entire miscue analysis procedure, clearly belong to K. Goodman, Y. Goodman, and Burke.

As you can see, the first column on the form is for the "text word;" the text word that the student read incorrectly should be written in this space.

The second column is for the "miscue"; the word (or non-word) that the student actually read should be written here (Note: if it is a non-word, try your best to spell it phonetically).

The third and fourth columns "High G/P or Low G/P" have to do with the graphophonic similarity of the oral reading miscue to the actual text word. If the oral reading miscue has 50 percent or more of the same letters as the text word, the miscue would be considered a high graphophonic miscue and a check (✔) should be placed in this column; conversely, if the miscue has less than 50 percent of the same letters as the text word, the miscue would be considered a low graphophonic miscue and a check (✔) should be placed in this column.

The fifth and sixth columns "Syn. Acc. or Syn. Unacc." have to do with the syntactic similarity of the oral reading miscue and the text word. Remember (see chapter 1) that *syntax* refers to word order or grammar; therefore, in order to decide whether a student's miscue is syntactically acceptable or syntactically unacceptable you simply have to ask yourself the following question: Does this miscue result in a syntactically acceptable sentence structure? (i.e., same part of speech in the case of "substitution miscues" or syntactically correct sentence structure in the case of "insertion miscues" [word added that is *not* in the text] or "omission miscues" [word deleted that *is* in the text]). If the answer to the aforementioned question is "yes," then a check should be placed in the "syn acc" column. If the answer to this question is "no", then a check should be placed in the "syn unacc" column.

The seventh and eighth columns "Sem. Acc. or Sem. Unacc." have to do with the semantic (i.e., meaning) acceptability or unacceptability of the oral reading miscue. If the miscue significantly distorts the author's intended meaning, the miscue would be considered a semantically unacceptable miscue and a check should be placed in this column; conversely, if the miscue does not significantly distort the author's intended message, then the miscue would be considered a semantically acceptable miscue and a check should be placed in this column. The ninth and tenth columns on the form, "S/C+ or S/C−" have to do with whether or not the student *self-corrected* the miscue (i.e., corrected the miscue without any feedback whatsoever from the teacher/listener) ; if the miscue was self-corrected, a check should be placed in the "S/C+" column; conversely, if the miscue was left uncorrected, a check should be placed in the "S/C–" column. "Clearly, students who consistently self-correct their meaning distorting miscues (i.e., semantically unacceptable miscues) ARE "self-monitoring" for meaning; this is an excellent text processing strategy. Conversely, students who rarely self-correct their semantically unacceptable/meaning distorting miscues are NOT self-monitoring for meaning as they read; they MUST be taught to do so! A "semantic prompt" from the teacher (e.g., "Does that make sense? Read the sentence again silently; if it doesn't make sense, see if you can decide *which* word made it NOT make sense; what word WOULD make sense in that sentence?") will be most helpful in this situation. Students who consistently fail to self-monitor and self-correct their meaning distorting miscues need to develop an "internal monitoring system." This can be facilitated through "reflective teacher feedback" (see above) to student miscue.

Let's try to analyze one oral reading miscue using the Modified Miscue Analysis Form as follows.

Table 3-2.

Miscue Analysis									
Text Word	miscue	high gp	low gp	syn acc	syn unacc	sem acc	sem un	sc +	sc –
(Joey) house	horse	✔		✔			✔		✔
(Susan) very large	huge					✔			✔
(Hector) good	———					✔			✔
(Meg) ceiling	selling	✔			✔		✔	✔	

Joey, a second-grade student, was reading the following sentence: "Mary had a big red house. It had a white door and a black roof." Joey made only one oral reading miscue: he read the word *house* as *horse*.

As you can see, column one, "text word" has the actual text word *house* written in it. Column two, "miscue," has the word *horse* written in it. Column three, "High G/P" has been checked indicating that this is a high graphophonic miscue (i.e., the miscue has more than 50 percent of the same letters as the text word). Column five, "Syn. Acc." has been checked indicating that this is a syntactically acceptable miscue (i.e., the text word house and the miscue horse are the same part of speech—nouns). Column eight, "Sem. Unacc." has been checked indicating that this is a semantically unacceptable miscue (this miscue significantly alters the author's intended meaning). And finally, column ten "S/C–" has been checked, indicating that Joey did not self-correct this miscue. Hence, in summary, when Joey substituted the word horse for the text word house, he actually made a high graphophonic, syntactically acceptable, semantically unacceptable miscue which he did not self-correct.

Obviously, the analysis of one miscue does not an assessment make! However, if Joey's reading over time is characterized by a majority of high graphophonic, syntactically acceptable, semantically unacceptable miscues, then it would be reasonable for the teacher to conclude the following: As Joey transacts with text:

1. he is most definitely using the graphophonic cueing system and is using it reasonably well (as evidenced by the large number of high graphophonic miscues);

2. he is using the syntactic cueing system reasonably well (as evidenced by the large number of syntactically acceptable miscues);

3. he is NOT using the semantic cueing system well at all (as evidenced by the large number of semantically unacceptable miscues); clearly, Joey lacks the most critical insight that a reader needs to have, that print/text has to make sense! (F. Smith, 1994);

4. he is not consistently self-monitoring himself as he reads; if he were doing so, he would have realized (especially after the second sentence) that the word horse did not make sense, and he would have self-corrected this meaning distorting miscue.

At this point, it is worth repeating Kenneth Goodman's point (K. Goodman, 1967): a student's miscues provide the teacher/listener with a "window on the reader's processing"; they allow the teacher/listener to see how the reader is transacting/interacting with the text . . . which cue systems he/she is using and which he/she may, in fact, not be using. Joey, for example, needs to be taught that "it has to make sense!" Stated differently, he has to learn how to self-monitor for meaning and how to better use the semantic cueing system as he attempts to process meaningful discourse. Proficient readers, by definition, have learned how to flexibly use all three cueing systems. Joey, on the other hand, seems to be somewhat fixated on the graphophonic cueing system; he is so focused on looking at letters and sounds (graphophonic cues) that he often fails to attend to meaning (semantics).

A few more examples may be helpful: Susan, a 5th grade student, was reading the following sentence: "The snake was the longest one he had ever seen; in fact, it was more than twenty feet long and more than ten inches in diameter. Josh was more than a little afraid. Could you blame him, this WAS a very large snake," Susan "miscued" on the words "very large"; she substituted the word "huge." This is called a "multiple word miscue." As you can see, the words "very large" are written in the Text Word column. Susan's miscue, "huge" has been written in the "miscue" column. Neither "high gp" or "low gp" have been checked since it is unnecessary to rate multiple word miscues for graphophonic similarity. A check has been placed in the "syn acc." column since the miscue results in an acceptable syntactic structure. A check has been placed in the "sem acc" column because this miscue does not significantly alter the author's intended meaning.

Hector, an 8th grade student, was reading the following text: "My dad's good friend, Joseph, told him several times not to be so concerned about getting overtime pay every week; sometimes it comes, sometimes it doesn't. Even though Joseph was dad's friend, dad had a very difficult time understanding this concept. He felt that he deserved to work overtime whenever he so desired." Hector "miscued" by omitting the word "good" in the second sentence of the text. Hence, the word "good" is placed in the Text Word column. He omitted the word "good"; therefore a blank line has been placed in the "miscue" column indicating that this was, in fact, an "omission miscue." The columns "high gp" and "low gp" are not checked since "omission miscues" cannot be rated in terms of their graphophonic resemblance to the text word. The "syn acc" column has been checked since this miscue resulted in an acceptable syntactic structure. The "sem acc" column has been checked since this miscue did not significantly change the meaning that the author intended to convey. The "sc-" column has been checked since Hector did not self-correct this miscue.

Meg, a 4th grade student, was reading the following text: "When my uncle Henry popped the cork, it made a loud noise; it almost made a hole in our ceiling." Meg initially "miscued" on the word "ceiling"; she read it as "selling." However, she realized her mistake and corrected herself and read the word correctly. The appropriate columns on Table 3-2 have been checked.

The following procedure should be used when conducting a "formal" miscue analysis of a student's reading:

1. Have the student read from a text that is at his/her reading instructional level (i.e., 90 percent or better word recognition accuracy and 70 percent or better comprehension);

2. Choose a passage for the student to read;

3. Give him/her an opportunity to read the passage silently;

4. Ask the student to read the same passage aloud, instructing him/her to simply do the best that he/she can on words that may give him/her difficulty, even skipping them if necessary;

5. Mark the student's oral reading deviations from print (miscues) on your copy of the text passage;

6. After the entire passage has been read aloud, ask the student to retell as much as he/she can about the text;

7. Rate the student's comprehension of the passage as "excellent," "satisfactory," or "unsatisfactory," based upon his/her retelling (Note: If you believe that the student may be reticent to engage in this unstructured retelling, you may ask some structured literal and interpretive reading comprehension questions; using this procedure you can quantitatively (e.g., 70 percent, 80 percent, 90 percent) assess the student's comprehension of the text in the following manner: 90 percent or above would be considered "excellent" comprehension; 70 percent–89 percent would be considered "satisfactory" comprehension; and less than 70 percent would be considered "unsatisfactory" comprehension;

8. Analyze the student's oral reading miscues using the "Modified Miscue Analysis Form."(Note: When conducting a "formal" miscue analysis, it is often recommended that the teacher tape record the student's oral reading; clearly, this provides the teacher with the flexibility of listening to the oral reading again at a later time.)

It is this author's firm belief that the miscue analysis procedure is an extremely valuable reading assessment technique; it allows the teacher to investigate not only the *product* of the student's reading (i.e., his/her comprehension of the text), but also the *process(es)* he/she is utilizing when attempting to construct meaning from written text. Unfortunately, even the Modified Miscue Analysis Form (discussed previously) can be somewhat time-consuming for the teacher. Therefore, I strongly recommend that teachers use the form only as a self-training instrument. Once they become even reasonably proficient at analyzing students' miscues by using the form, they should strive to engage in, what I like to call, "Mental Miscue Analysis" (MMA) (Cavuto, 2001). Every time any student in class reads aloud from text, the teacher should mentally analyze that student's miscues by simply asking THREE questions:

1. Is the miscue semantically acceptable (i.e., meaning retaining) or semantically unacceptable (i.e., meaning distorting)? (Note: this question *must* be asked first since meaning is always the most important aspect of any language activity);

2. If the miscue was semantically unacceptable, did the reader self-correct the miscue?

3. Is the miscue high graphophonic (i.e., looks and/or sounds like the text word) or low graphophonic? (i.e., does not look and/or sound like the text word).*

If teachers initially concentrate on asking themselves the first two questions only ("Is it semantically acceptable or unacceptable?"; "Did he/she self-correct?") they will see that Mental Miscue Analysis (MMA) is not only do-able, it is much easier, less intrusive, and less time-consuming than the more formal procedures outlined above (e.g., audiotaping students' oral reading and filling in Modified

Miscue Analysis Forms.) Clearly, teachers shouldn't totally abandon the use of Modified Miscue Analysis Forms; they do provide tangible evidence of a student's reading processes as reflected by his/her miscues; however, by conducting Mental Miscue Analyses over time, the teacher is constantly observing and analyzing. Keeping an anecdotal record of the types of miscues a particular student makes over the course of a school year (based upon the teacher's ongoing MMA) would be a very naturalistic, valid indicator of the child's reading processing strategies.

It should also be pointed out that there are many students who have excellent word recognition/decoding accuracy but very poor reading comprehension. Generally speaking, for these students, a miscue analysis will not be very revealing of strategies at all; there will be very few, if any miscues, to analyze! Also, as with all assessment, patterns are far more important than individual cases; hence, teachers should strive to discern miscue patterns rather than concentrate on or debate the rating of one or two miscues.

In conclusion, miscues are a natural result of the integration of text-based information and reader background knowledge. Reading involves a transaction between the reader and the text; the text contains three language cueing systems; the reader brings his/her background knowledge to the print in order to construct meaning. Students' miscues provide us with important information about their processing strategies; hence, it is critically important that teachers become as proficient as possible at conducting both formal and informal (e.g., Mental Miscue Analysis [MMA]) miscue analyses as part of their naturalistic, classroom-based, reading assessment repertoire of strategies.

*NOTE: When readers omit a text word (omission miscue) or add a word to the text (insertion miscue), these miscues cannot be rated as either high or low graphophonic; they can, however, be rated for their semantic acceptability/unacceptability.

MISCUE PATTERNS

- A pattern of high graphophonic, syntactically acceptable, semantically unacceptable miscues (that remain uncorrected) is usually indicative of a reader who has adequate knowledge of grapheme/phoneme relationships (i.e., knows letter-sound relationships "reasonably" well); this is suggested by the preponderance of high graphophonic miscues. This reader also has a sense that text has to sound like "real language"; this is suggested by the fact that a majority of his/her miscues are syntactically (i.e., grammatically) acceptable. Unfortunately, this kind of reader lacks the most critical insight that one needs to be a proficient reader: text has to make sense! (Smith, 1994).This reader's pattern of semantically unacceptable miscues significantly distorts the author's intended meaning; hence, when this reader finishes reading, his/her comprehension of the text is usually inadequate. Not only do his/her miscues significantly distort the meaning of the text, the fact that he/she does not even make an attempt to self-correct them clearly indicates that he/she is not consistently self-monitoring for meaning as he/she reads. Simply stated, this kind of reader is overutilizing the graphophonic cueing system and underutilizing the semantic cueing system. He/she is on a "word search" rather than a "meaning search." This reader is also doing too much "bottom-up processing" and not enough "top-down processing." He/she is focusing his/her attention on the "surface structure" of text rather than on its "deep structure" (Chomsky, 1957).

- A pattern of low graphophonic, a combination of syntactically acceptable and syntactically unacceptable, and semantically unacceptable miscues usually indicates a reader who either has poor knowledge of grapheme-phoneme relationships or is consistently failing to apply his/her knowledge of grapheme-phoneme relationships. [Note: This is a very important differentiation to make. A simple informal or formal assessment of symbol-sound knowledge would help the teacher decide whether the problem is really a lack of phonic knowledge or simply the student's inability to consistently apply the knowledge of letter/sound knowledge that he/she does, in fact, possess.] This kind of pattern is also characteristic of a reader who is not reading for meaning (deep structure). The semantically unacceptable miscues that remain uncorrected also indicate a student who is not self-monitoring for meaning as he/she attempts to process printed information.

- A pattern of a combination of low graphophonic and high graphophonic miscues that are syntactically and semantically acceptable is usually indicative of a reader who is flexibly using all three cueing systems (i.e., graphophonic, syntactic and semantic). This reader has an adequate knowledge of grapheme-phoneme relationships; however, as he/she is interacting/transacting with text, the combination of bottom-up and top-down strategies results in miscues. The fact that the miscues are both syntactically and semantically acceptable would suggest that this reader is most definitely reading for meaning (i.e., processing text at a deep structure level).

Unfortunately, the teacher who is not trained in "miscue analysis" may, in fact, believe that this reader is "doing something wrong." Teachers who adhere to a model of reading that suggests that proficient readers read every word exactly as it is written on the page will, invariably, believe that this reader needs to be corrected; by so doing, they are taking a reader who is processing text at a deep structure (i.e., meaning) level and forcing him to become overly preoccupied with surface structure accuracy; this could most certainly be counterproductive. Teachers have said to me, "What should I do then, just let these miscues remain uncorrected? What are the other students going to think?" My response is always the same: Teach your students about how reading works; share your knowledge of the process with them. Let them understand that your feedback to miscues is not arbitrary but rather informed by your in-depth understanding of the process. If this is done on a regular basis, it is quite possible that students, even as young as 1st and 2nd grade, will be able to say, "Ms. Jenkins, I know why you didn't correct Shawn when he read 'big' for 'large,' because it didn't change the meaning. Shawn did that because he was thinking ahead as he reads—that's a good thing to do!'" This is indeed possible, however, it must be taught. I like to refer to this as making our students "privy to process." Yetta Goodman has developed a strategy called "retrospective miscue analysis" where students learn to discuss and analyze their own miscues as a way of becoming more cognizant of their reading processes/strategies (Y. Goodman, 1996).

- A pattern of low graphophonic miscues (or a combination of low and high graphophonic miscues) that are syntactically and semantically acceptable that are almost always self-corrected would indicate a reader who is processing text at a deep structure (meaning) level; his/her miscues tend to preserve the author's intended meaning. Clearly, this reader is maximizing the use of semantic and syntactic cues as he/she processes text and is using only as much graphophonic information as if necessary in order to make a reasonable decision. This kind of reader is said to be "perceptually parsimonious" (Gibson and Levin, 1975). He/she is engaging in much top-down processing (i.e., predicting that which is coming next in the text based upon text-based and schema-based information). Why, then, one might reasonably ask, does this reader "almost always" self-correct his/her miscues?; they don't distort the author's intended meaning (they are semantically acceptable). In my teaching experience, this type of behavior is oftentimes a "conditioned effect" (Skinner, 1938). This reader has internalized the *erroneous conclusion,* either through teacher or parent/caretaker feedback, that in order to be a proficient reader, one must read every word exactly as its written on the page (see the preceding paragraph re: the counterproductive nature of this kind of feedback).

There are numerous permutations of the patterns described above. As one begins to master the art of Mental Miscue Analysis (MMA) (Cavuto, 2001) as one means of naturalistically assessing readers' processing strategies, different patterns will emerge for each student in the class; however, generally speaking, the patterns should resemble one of the four discussed above. Remember—Miscue Analysis is only effective if the student miscues as he/she processes text. If the student has excellent word identification/decoding accuracy, he/she will make very few, if any, miscues. Hence, they will provide the teacher with very limited information about the student's processing strategies. As was mentioned earlier in this chapter, for this kind of student, an informal assessment of his/her reading comprehension (e.g., by asking him/her to retell the most salient points made in the text) would be a much more valid assessment; this retelling is, in fact, an important part of the miscue analysis procedure. This is not to suggest, however, that teachers should ignore the few miscues made by "excellent decoders/poor comprehenders." It is not unusual that if/when these readers do miscue, the miscue is semantically unacceptable and it remains uncorrected. This type of reading behavior would provide the teacher with additional evidence that this student is clearly not reading for meaning and has not learned self-monitoring skills/strategies.

FOLLOW-UP EXERCISES

1. Frankie is a fourth grade student. His teacher has noted the following about Frankie's oral reading miscues: they are usually high graphophonic; they are syntactically acceptable; they are almost always semantically unacceptable; he never self-corrects his miscues; and, he miscues often when reading his social studies, science, and language arts texts. Based upon this limited information, answer the following questions:

    Question 1: What does this kind of miscue pattern reveal about Frankie's reading strategies? (specifically, which cueing systems are Frankie using/not using as he attempts to process printed discourse?) Explain your answer.

    Question 2: Is Frankie reading on a deep structure or a surface structure level? Explain your answer.

    Question 3: Does Frankie self-monitor as he reads? Explain your answer.

    Question 4: Do you think that Frankie has adequate/inadequate comprehension after reading his grade level texts? Explain your answer.

2. The following Modified Miscue Analysis Form (Table 3-3) has several of Sonja's miscues analyzed. Sonja's teacher has indicated that these miscues are consistent with a pattern of miscues that she has observed over the entire semester (i.e., using Mental Miscue Analysis [MMA]).

Table 3-3.

Miscue Analysis—Sonja									
Text Word	miscue	high gp	low gp	syn acc	syn unacc	sem acc	sem un	sc +	sc –
house	horse	✔		✔			✔		
shorts	shots	✔		✔			✔		✔
friends	frinds	✔			✔		✔		✔
street	streep	✔			✔		✔		✔
rain	ran	✔			✔		✔		✔
kitchen	kitten	✔		✔			✔		✔
soup	soap	✔		✔			✔		✔
father	fatter	✔			✔		✔		✔
hopping	hoping	✔		✔			✔		✔
garage	grage	✔			✔		✔		✔
		$\frac{10}{10}$	$\frac{0}{10}$	$\frac{5}{10}$	$\frac{5}{10}$	$\frac{0}{10}$	$\frac{10}{10}$	0	$\frac{9}{10}$
		100%	0%	50%	50%	0%	100%		90%

Answer the following questions based upon this "formal" analysis of Sonja's miscues:

Question 1: Does Sonja appear to have adequate/inadequate knowledge of grapheme/phoneme relationships? Explain your answer.

Yes. every miscue was high graphonic

Question 2: Based upon this analysis, what can you tell about Sonja's reading comprehension? Her listening comprehension? Explain your answer.

She has a pretty good reading comprehension because she self-corrects nine of her ten miscues. Not enough information for listening comp.

Question 3: Is Sonja self-monitoring as she reads? Explain your answer.

Yes. She is Self correcting

Question 4: Does Sonja appear to have the "insight" that the language that she produces as she attempts to process printed discourse should sound like "real" language? Explain your answer.

Yes. She uses a few nonsense words but self-corrects them often.

3. Ralph, a seventh-grade student, usually reads his textbooks silently; however, Mr. Fletcher, Ralph's social studies teacher, believes that it is worthwhile to have his students take turns reading aloud from the textbook during class time; Ralph, an "A" student in social studies finds this to be a particularly stressful activity. When it is Ralph's turn to read aloud, he often miscues; every time he does so, Mr. Fletcher immediately corrects Ralph, telling him "Slow down, be more careful!" There is definitely a pattern to Ralph's miscues: they tend to be low graphophonic and semantically acceptable. On those rare occasions when Ralph makes a semantically unacceptable miscue, he attempts to self-correct it; however, usually Mr. Fletcher doesn't give him an opportunity to do so and says the text word aloud himself. Answer the following questions based upon this limited information:

Question 1: Why do you think Ralph finds this to be a "particularly stressful" activity? Explain your answer.

Question 2: Do you think that Ralph has adequate/inadequate schemata to bring to the social studies text? Yes? No? Not enough information to make a decision? Explain your answer.

Question 3: Does Ralph appear to engage in more top-down or more bottom-up processing as he reads his social studies text? Explain your answer.

Question 4: Does Mr. Fletcher's "feedback" to Ralph's miscues encourage more "surface structure processing" or more "deep structure processing?" Explain your answer.

4. Jenny (a third-grader) read the following passage from her social studies text and made the *oral reading miscues* as indicated (i.e., in italics above text word) :

The Slave Girl

(1) *dutiful*
This little girl was born in 1821. She was a beautiful little girl with black skin and big, black eyes.

(2) *prints*   (3) *saves*   (4) *save*   (5) *about*
Her parents were slaves and she was a slave, too. She was not allowed to do what she wanted.

(6) *odors*   (7) *onned*
She had to take orders from the people who owned her. She was not allowed to learn to read

(8) *heated*   (9) *save* (10) *taught*
and write. She hated being a slave and thought that all people should be free. She ran away from

(11) *saves*   (12) *farmers*
home and showed other slaves how to escape as well. She became very, very famous for helping

(13) *saves*   (14) *free-dome*
slaves escape to freedom.

Question 1: Analyze Jenny's miscues using a Modified Miscue Analysis Form.

Question 2: Based upon this analysis, which cueing system does Jenny appear to be over-utilizing? Which one does she appear to be under-utilizing? Explain your answers.

graphophonic-over
semantic-under.

Question 3: Is Jenny a bottom-up or a top-down reader? Explain your answer.

Question 4: Based upon your analysis of Jenny's miscues, do you believe that her reading comprehension of the social studies passage that she read was adequate or inadequate? Explain your answer.

References

Betts, E.A. (1946). *Foundations of Reading Instruction.* New York: American Book Company.

Cavuto, George J. (2001). "Mental Miscue Analysis (MMA): Developing the 'Knowing Ear.'" Manuscript submitted for publication.

Chomsky, N. (1957). *Syntactic Structures.* The Hague: Mouton, 1957.

Gibson, E.J. & Levin, H. (1975). *The Psychology of Reading.* Cambridge, MA: MIT Press.

Goodman, K.S. (1967). "Reading: A Psycholinguistic Guessing Game." *Journal of the Reading Specialist,* 6, 126–135.

Goodman, Yetta M. (1996). "Revaluing Readers while Readers Revalue Themselves: Retrospective Miscue Analysis." *The Reading Teacher,* 49, 600–609.

Goodman, Yetta M., & Burke, Carolyn L. (1972). *Reading Miscue Inventory Manual: Procedure for Diagnosis and Evaluation.* New York: Macmillan.

Skinner, B.F. (1938). *The Behavior of Organisms.* Englewood Cliffs, NJ: Prentice-Hall.

Smith, Frank. (1994). *Understanding Reading* (5th ed.). Hillsdale, NJ: Lawrence Erlbaum Assoc., Inc.

CHAPTER 4

Receptive Vocabulary

Key Words/Terms

receptive vocabulary, expressive vocabulary, word knowledge, linguistic competence, linguistic performance, language arts, receptive language skills, expressive language skills

When we talk about a person's vocabulary, we should be very specific in differentiating between his/her *receptive vocabulary* (the words that he/she knows the meanings of) and *expressive vocabulary* (the words that he/she uses). This differentiation is very important. Linguists talk about *linguistic competence* and *linguistic performance*. The former refers to an individual's internalized knowledge of his/her native language; the latter refers to an individual's ability to use that internalized knowledge to generate coherent speech/language. Hence, receptive vocabulary is considered part of one's linguistic competence, whereas, expressive vocabulary is considered part of one's linguistic performance.

When we think about the four language arts (i.e., reading, writing, listening, and speaking), it is a simple task to divide them into *receptive language skills* and *expressive language skills*. Reading and listening are considered receptive language activities; writing and speaking are considered expressive language activities. For this reason, a reader's receptive vocabulary (i.e., the storehouse of words of which one knows the meanings) will have a much greater impact on his/her reading comprehension than will his/her expressive vocabulary. Similarly, a listener's receptive vocabulary will have a much greater impact on how much he/she has understood than will his/her expressive vocabulary. When a person speaks or writes, he/she is using his/her expressive vocabulary; hence, an individual's expressive vocabulary will influence his/her ability to communicate orally (i.e., speak) or in written form (write). For the aforementioned reasons, receptive vocabulary is considered to be an integral part of the reading process; therefore, it is part of our Simple Reading Assessment Model (S-RAM) (see Figure 4-1).

Figure 4-1. Simple Reading Assessment Model (S-Ram).

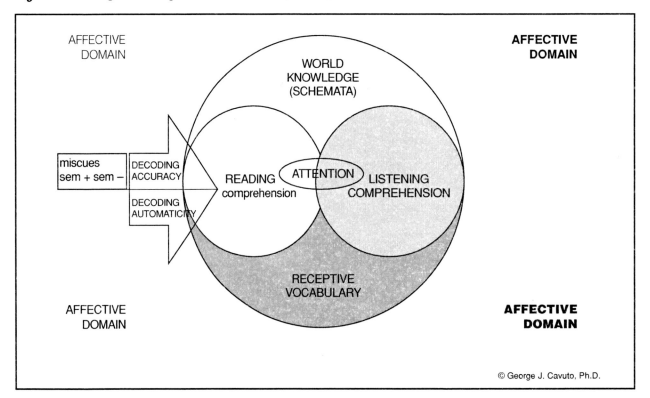

What does it mean to know what a word means? Researchers have pondered this question for the past century. Researchers (Beck and McKeown, 1991) have suggested that there are four stages of word (vocabulary) knowledge:

- Stage 1—never saw it before;

- Stage 2—heard it but doesn't know what it means;

- Stage 3—recognizes it in context as having something to do with . . . ;

- Stage 4—knows it well.

For the purposes of our Simple Reading Assessment Model (S-RAM), we are going to say that a particular word is part of a reader's receptive vocabulary if he/she knows, reasonably well, what the word means, even when it is presented out of context. By *reasonably well*, we mean that the student knows the word well enough that he/she can demonstrate this knowledge with a definition, an explanation, an example, an illustration, or by providing a situational context for the word. For example, if the teacher asks the class if anyone knows what the word obnoxious means and Heather replies, "Yes, it's what Joey was being to the substitute yesterday," clearly, the word obnoxious is part of Heather's receptive vocabulary.

Reading research (Beck and McKeown, 1991) has consistently indicated that *word knowledge* (i.e., receptive vocabulary) correlates very well with reading comprehension. Clearly, this does *not* mean that simply because a reader may know the meaning of every word on a page of his/her social studies text that he/she will necessarily have understood the author's intended meaning. Indeed, we have learned that, in reading, as in most human activities, the *whole is often greater than the sum of its parts*. A student who is not actively engaged during the reading process can know the meaning of all of the words on a page and finish reading the page with the feeling that he/she has not read it at all (i.e., with no reading comprehension whatsoever!) Adequate receptive vocabulary vis-à-vis that which is to be read by no means guarantees satisfactory reading comprehension; however, if a reader comes to a page of text and encounters many words on the page that he/she does not know the meanings of, this will definitely have a negative impact on his/her comprehension of the information presented on that page.

The best way to assess students' receptive vocabularies is by ongoing, naturalistic, classroom-based assessment. There are numerous opportunities during the school day to informally assess your students' receptive vocabularies. These include, but are by no means limited to, the following: during or after a literature book (or chapter) has been read to the class; during the pre-reading activities that are done prior to having the class read a chapter in a content area textbook; during classroom discussions following the reading of a chapter of content area textbook; as students are discussing a piece of literature read during a literature circle; by analyzing students' use of vocabulary in their written expression (note: this analysis would be of the students' expressive vocabulary ; however, oftentimes, a rich and varied expressive vocabulary may be reflective of a well-developed receptive vocabulary); and last, but by no means least, through teacher-generated questions.

If, after using some of the aforementioned observational techniques, you decide that a particular student in your class has a weakness in his/her receptive vocabulary, you should place a minus (–) sign in the receptive vocabulary section of the Reading Assessment Model [Figure 4-2].

Conversely, if your ongoing observations over time clearly indicate that a student in your class has a strength in receptive vocabulary, you should place a plus (+) sign in the receptive vocabulary section of the Simple Reading Assessment Model (S-RAM). Whether receptive vocabulary is a strength or a weakness for a particular student, I would strongly recommend that you include in the receptive vocabulary section of the S-RAM some of the specific words that he/she knew/did not know that led you to draw this conclusion about his/her receptive vocabulary. This kind of simple, anecdotal record will be very helpful when you discuss each student's reading strengths and weaknesses with his/her parents/caretakers and when you discuss these with the student himself/herself.

If a student has a rather significant deficiency in his/her receptive vocabulary we could reasonably assume that his/her reading comprehension and listening comprehension skills will be deficient as well. As was stated above, if a reader does not know the meanings of a significant number of words on a page of text

Figure 4-2. Simple Reading Assessment Model (S-Ram).

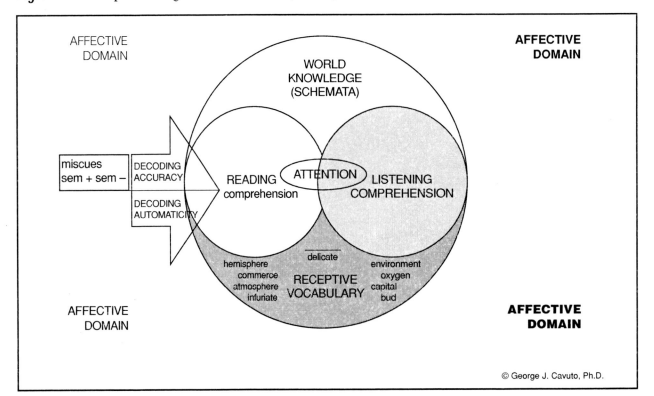

(particularly if these words are critical to the concepts being presented), it will be very difficult/impossible for him/her to understand the page of text (Johnson and Pearson, 1984). Similarly, if a student finds many of the words used by the teacher during a science lecture to be unfamiliar, his/her listening comprehension following that lecture will most likely be unsatisfactory. Receptive vocabulary is critical to understanding, regardless of the mode of processing (i.e., visual or auditory).

Reading is a receptive language act and, as such, the reader's receptive vocabulary will have a significant influence on both the reading comprehension process (i.e., how the reader attempts to comprehend text) and the reading comprehension product (i.e., how much the reader has understood about the text that he/she has read).

FOLLOW-UP EXERCISES

Directions: Read the following scenarios and answer the questions that follow.

1. Michael is in the fourth grade. His classroom teacher has observed that Michael almost always has his hand up when she asks, "Who knows what that word means?" (and indeed, he knows the correct meaning). She has also noticed that Michael likes to experiment with words as he writes.

    Question #1: Would you put a plus (+) or a minus (–) in the receptive vocabulary section in Michael's Simple Reading Assessment Model (S-RAM)? Explain your answer.

    Question #2: Based upon the limited information presented, do you believe that Michael is a good reading comprehender, a poor reading comprehender, or is there insufficient information to make a reasonable guess? Explain your answer.

    Question #3: Based upon the limited information presented, do you believe that Michael has adequate word identification/decoding accuracy, inadequate word identification/decoding accuracy, or is there insufficient information to make a reasonable guess? Explain your answer.

Question #4: Based upon the limited information presented, do you believe that Michael has adequate listening comprehension skills, poor listening comprehension skills, or is there insufficient information to make a reasonable guess? Explain your answer.

Question #5: Based upon the limited information presented, do you believe that Michael has adequate decoding automaticity, inadequate decoding automaticity, or is there insufficient information to make a reasonable guess? Explain your answer.

Question #6: Based upon the limited information presented, do you believe that Michael is predisposed to being a top-down processor of text, a bottom-up processor of text, or is there insufficient information to make a reasonable guess?

Question #7: Based upon the limited information presented, what can you tell about Michael's basic sight word storehouse (i.e., his basic sight vocabulary)? Explain your answer.

Question #8: Based upon the limited information presented, which cueing systems should Michael be able to use quite well as he attempts to process printed discourse? Explain your answer.

2. Carina is a tenth-grade student. Her English teacher has observed that Carina oftentimes seems confused as to the meanings of words. The class is reading Steinbeck's novel *Of Mice and Men* and Carina seems to be struggling with the vocabulary. On several occasions she indicated to the teacher, with frustration in her voice, "I don't know what that word means."

Question #1: Based upon the limited information presented, would you consider receptive vocabulary to be a strength or a weakness for Carina? Explain your answer.

Question #2: Based upon the limited information presented, what reasonable guess would you make about Carina's reading comprehension skills? Explain your answer.

Question #3: Based upon the limited information presented, would Carina perform significantly better during classroom discussions if the teacher read the book aloud to the class? Explain your answer.

Question #4: Based upon the limited information presented, what conclusions could you draw, if any, about Carina's word identification/decoding accuracy and Carina's word identification/decoding automaticity? Explain your answer.

Question #5: Based upon the limited information presented, what conclusions could you draw, if any, about Carina's world knowledge/schemata? Explain your answer.

3. Billy is a second-grade student. His teacher has made the following observations over time: Billy is very curious about the meanings of words; whenever he hears a word that he doesn't know, he makes it a point to ask about its meaning. During literature discussions, when questions are raised about the meaning of a particular word in the text, Billy is the first to raise his hand and he almost always answers correctly. Billy struggles to read his second-grade (2-1) basal reader. He makes many miscues and they tend to be meaning distorting. He rarely self-corrects these miscues. The other children in the class "moan and sigh" when Billy is called upon to read out loud.

    Question #1: Based upon the above information, would you place a plus (+) or a minus (–) in the receptive vocabulary section of the Simple Reading Assessment Model (S-RAM) for Billy? Explain your answer.

    Question #2: Based upon the above information, is word identification/decoding accuracy a strength or a weakness for Billy? Explain your answer.

    Question #3: Based upon the above information, is word identification/decoding automaticity a strength or a weakness for Billy? Explain your answer.

    Question #4: Based upon the above information, would you guess that Billy has adequate reading comprehension, inadequate reading comprehension, or do you believe that there is insufficient information to make a reasonable guess? Explain your answer.

Question #5: Based upon the above information, would you guess that Billy enjoys reading his homework assignments (i.e., from his textbooks) to his parents or does he prefer when they read the texts to him? Explain your answer.

Question #6: Based upon the above information, would you guess that Billy has above average intelligence, average intelligence, below average intelligence, or do you believe that there is insufficient information given to make a reasonable guess? Explain your answer.

Question #7: Which is better, Billy's receptive vocabulary or his basic sight vocabulary? Explain your answer.

Question #8: Has Billy learned to self-monitor when he reads? Explain your answer.

REFERENCES

Beck, Isabel and McKeown, Margaret (1991). "Conditions of vocabulary acquisition." In Rebecca Barr, Michael L. Kamil, Peter Mosenthal, and P. David Pearson (Eds.), *Handbook of Reading Research: Volume II* (pp. 789–814).

Johnson, D.D. and Pearson, P.D. (1984). *Teaching Reading Vocabulary.* New York: Holt, Rinehart, and Winston.

CHAPTER 5

World Knowledge/Schemata

Key Words/Terms

world knowledge, background knowledge, experiential background, schemata, nonvisual information, visual information, schema, global predictions, focal predictions, constructing meaning, reader-text transaction, perceptual parsimony, theory of the world (Smith), schema instantiation, auding

World Knowledge, also referred to as background knowledge, experiential background, schemata, nonvisual information (Smith,1994) may be defined as the reader's sum total knowledge of the world. This knowledge may have been gained through *actual experiences* (e.g., everyday life experiences, taking trips) or *vicarious experiences* (e.g., reading books, watching movies). The way in which the reader gained the knowledge is not critical; what is important, is that the reader has this knowledge. Clearly, there are significant differences in readers' world knowledge/experiential backgrounds. Some have more, some have less. Some have more on certain topics (e.g., dinosaurs), some have more on other topics (e.g., car engines).

Reading research has clearly established the importance of reader background knowledge (schemata) in reading comprehension (Anderson and Pearson, 1984). Much of this research confirms the constructive nature of the reading process: readers do not simply engage in a passive extraction of meaning from the printed page; instead, they actively employ strategies that allow them to accurately reconstruct the author's intended meaning (Cooper, 1993). One such active processing strategy involves using existing background knowledge (schema/schemata) to make predictions as to what is coming next in the text. This donating from background knowledge to set up expectations as to what is going to come next in the text is called *prediction.* Active readers are constantly predicting/anticipating that which is going to come next in the text. Indeed, Smith suggests that readers make both global predictions and focal predictions (Smith, 1994). A *global prediction*, for example, might involve guessing what a book will be about based on the title and cover illustration; predicting the content of the text to come at the paragraph, sentence, or even word level would be examples of *focal predictions.*

[Note: It is very important to point out at this juncture that when we use the word *guess* in the above context, we are by no means talking about a random, haphazard, shot-in-the dark kind of conjecturing. Instead, we are talking about a very sophisticated cognitive, constructive process that the reader engages in as he/she is transacting with the text. This type of guessing requires the reader to flexibly use all of the textual information (i.e., graphophonic, semantic, and syntactic cues) and interface these with his/her topic specific background/world knowledge (i.e., schema) to construct a reasonable hypothesis re: the author's intended meaning and to then extend this hypothesis to predict that which is going to be presented next. Those literacy experts who frown on guessing during the reading process should be reminded that intelligent, informed, guessing gets most of us through every day of our lives! Without making predictions (i.e., guessing), we would require so much information that we would experience information overload. As Smith suggests (Smith, 1994, p. 8), our world knowledge, our theory of the world, is our "shield against bewilderment." It allows us to function quite efficiently without the necessity of being given all of the information. Indeed, it allows us to be perceptually parsimonious (Gibson and Levin, 1975).]

Because of the reciprocal relationship that exists between *nonvisual information* (i.e., world knowledge/schemata) and *visual information* (i.e., textual information) (see chapter 1), readers who have an abundance of world knowledge will be predisposed to being better reading comprehenders than readers who have a paucity of world knowledge. Why do we say predisposed? It is quite possible for a reader to have exceptional background knowledge to bring to text and yet, for several reasons (which will be discussed later in this text), fail to do so. Sometimes this is referred to as a failure to instantiate existing schema (Anderson and Pearson, 1984). Conversely, it is impossible for a reader to instantiate schema that is not there: for example, a reader who has limited schema about the human circulation system and is attempting to read the chapter in the eighth-grade science textbook about the human circulation system, will not be able to do lots of predicting (top-down processing). Just the opposite, he/she will have to rely on much text-based (i.e., bottom-up) processing which will make comprehending the text that much more difficult.

When the reader makes a prediction as to that which is going to come next in a text based upon the previously read text and his/her world knowledge, we say the reader has engaged in "top-down processing" (the reader has donated information to the page from his/her existing world knowledge). Researchers (K. Goodman, 1967; Smith, 1994) have found a positive correlation between a reader's ability to predict and his/ her reading comprehension. Clearly, since a reader makes his/her predictions from his/her world knowledge, readers with expansive world knowledge will be predisposed to engaging in much predicting (i.e., top-down processing) as they read different kinds of texts; readers with a paucity of world knowledge will have significant difficulty predicting (i.e., engaging in top-down processing); these readers will be forced to engage in much bottom-up processing (i.e., text based, non-anticipatory processing). Bottom-up processing is slower (i.e., less automatic) than top-down processing and oftentimes results in less than adequate comprehension of the text. Simply stated, it is very difficult to understand text if we have absolutely no background to bring to the text! Is it possible? Yes it is; however, it will be a time-consuming, labor intensive task.

There are numerous ways that teachers can evaluate their students' world knowledge/schemata using naturalistic, classroom-based, ongoing assessment techniques. Since world knowledge and receptive vocabulary correlate so well, the observational situations enumerated in chapter 4 for informally observing receptive vocabulary (e.g., during or after a literature book [or chapter] has been read to the class; during the pre-reading activities that are done prior to having the class read a chapter in a content area textbook; during classroom discussions following the reading of a chapter of a content area textbook; as students are discussing a piece of literature read during a literature circle; by analyzing students' use of vocabulary in their written expression) are as appropriate to informally assess students' world knowledge.

If, after using some of the aforementioned observational techniques, you decide that a particular student in your class has significant gaps in his/her world knowledge/schemata, you should place a minus (–) sign in the world knowledge section of the Simple Reading Assessment Model (S-RAM) (see Figure 5-1).

Figure 5-1. Simple Reading Assessment Model (S-Ram).

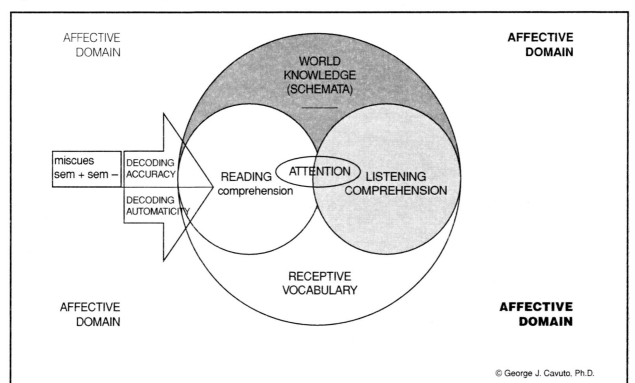

Conversely, if your ongoing observations over time clearly indicate that a student in your class has age/grade appropriate world knowledge you should place a plus (+) sign in the world knowledge section of the Simple Reading Assessment Model (S-RAM). (See Figure 5-2.)

Whether world knowledge is a strength or a weakness for a particular student, as with receptive vocabulary, I would once again strongly recommend that you include in the circle some anecdotal evidence of the specific background knowledge gaps that you noticed as part of your ongoing observation/assessment of this student's reading that led you to draw this conclusion about his/her world knowledge/experiential background. (See Figure 5-3.)

If a student has significant gaps in his/her world knowledge, we could reasonably hypothesize that his/her reading comprehension will be deficient as well. As has been stated previously in this text, reading involves a transaction between the reader and the text. The reader brings information to the text (top-down processing) and uses this information to make predictions about the text; simultaneously, the reader is extracting information from the text (bottom-up processing). Readers with significant gaps in their world knowledge will find reading most text to be a tedious, laborious, bottom-up, text-based process which ultimately lacks fruition. They will, in more cases than not, read and not understand that which

Figure 5-2. Simple Reading Assessment Model (S-Ram).

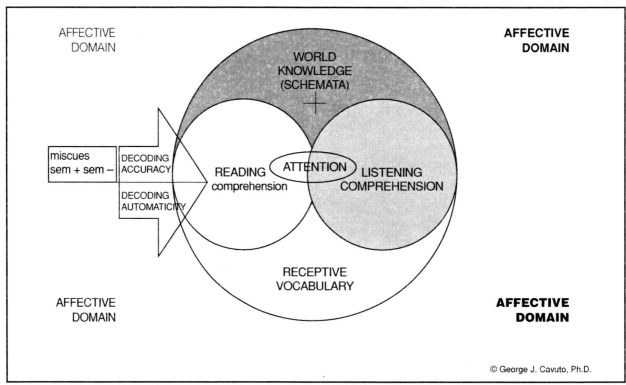

© George J. Cavuto, Ph.D.

Figure 5-3. Simple Reading Assessment Model (S-Ram).

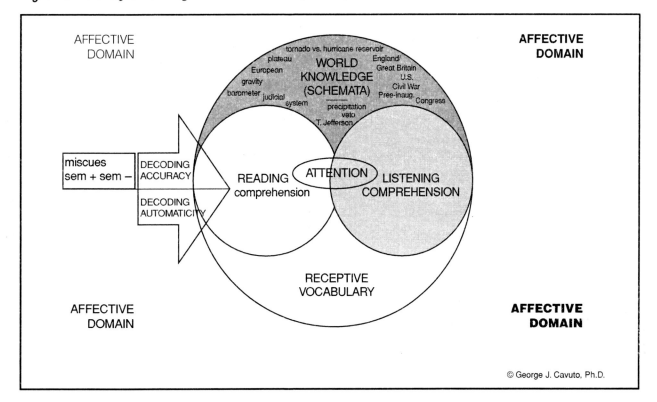

they have read. Conversely, readers who have adequate world knowledge to bring to the page are predisposed to being good reading comprehenders *if* they instantiate their world knowledge as they read *and* have adequate word identification/decoding accuracy and adequate word identification/decoding automaticity.

Similarly, if a student has significant gaps in his/her world knowledge, we could reasonably hypothesize that his/her listening comprehension will also be deficient. As a student is attempting to comprehend his/her teacher's lecture or, perhaps, a book that he/she is reading to the class, he/she is engaging in a listening comprehension activity, also referred to as *auding* (Brown, 1954). If the teacher is lecturing about the Civil War in the United States, for example, and the student lacks an age/grade appropriate U.S. Civil War schema, he/she will most certainly have difficulty comprehending the lecture; he will not be able to engage in active, predictive behaviors (i.e., predicting/constructing the teacher's message as he/she is delivering it) nor will he/she be able to relate the incoming information to an existing knowledge base (i.e., world knowledge). As will be discussed in more detail later in this text, the ability to relate *new* information to *known* information is a critical component of all comprehension activities.

FOLLOW-UP EXERCISES

Directions: Read the following scenarios and answer the questions that follow.

1. Sasha, a tenth-grade student, is having significant difficulty comprehending her world history textbook. Sasha's social studies' teacher has made the following classroom-based observations of Sasha's academic performance:

   • Sasha seems to have little knowledge/understanding of many of the critical concepts presented in class; this is evident during brainstorming sessions that precede the introduction of new material, when I ask her specific questions about terms/concepts/events introduced this term, or material that she should have learned in previous courses, during class discussions; and her performance on chapter and unit tests;

   • Sasha enjoys reading out loud from the social studies text in class; whenever I ask for a volunteer, Sasha is the first to raise her hand. Her oral reading is reasonably fast and fluent; she seldom stumbles over or misses a word;

   • Sasha's social studies journal entries (e.g., summary of text chapter, reaction to an event in the chapter, prediction as to what is going to happen in the next chapter) are very sparse—she writes a sentence or two.

   Question #1: Would you put a plus (+) or a minus (−) in the world knowledge section of Sasha's Reading Assessment Model (S-RAM) ? Explain your answer.

   Question #2: Based upon the information presented, what would you conclude about Sasha's receptive vocabulary (i.e., is it adequate/inadequate, or is there not enough information presented to draw a reasonable conclusion)?

Question #3: Based upon the information presented, would you put a plus (+) or a minus (−) in the word identification/decoding accuracy section of Sasha's Simple Reading Assessment Model (S-RAM)? Explain your answer. Would you put a plus (+) or a minus (−) in the word identification/decoding automaticity section of Sasha's Simple Reading Assessment Model (S-RAM)? Explain your answer.

Question #4: Would you put a plus (+) or a minus (−) in the reading comprehension section of Sasha's Simple Reading Assessment Model (S-RAM)? Explain your answer.

Question #5: As Sasha attempts to read her social studies textbook, does she engage in more top-down processing or more bottom-up processing ? Explain your answer.

Question #6: Being very much aware of her frustration in reading her Social Studies text and answering the chapter questions that follow, Sasha's parents have decided to read the text to her. Will this help her to better comprehend the text and answer the chapter questions? Explain your answer. Would you recommend that they continue this practice? Explain your answer.

Question #7: One of Sasha's teachers, fully realizing that she has a rather serious "reading problem," recommended that her parents look into purchasing a well-advertised, commercial "phonics program" for Sasha. Do you believe that this suggestion has merit? Explain your answer.

2. Jack is a fifth-grade student. His classroom teacher has observed the following: "Jack has significant difficulty identifying words as he reads his content area textbooks (i.e., science and social studies); he miscues often (making approximately an equal number of semantically acceptable miscues and semantically unacceptable miscues; even the words that he does decode correctly take him an inordinate amount of time to read. I'm amazed that Jack's reading comprehension is as good as it is! He answers the end-of-chapter questions reasonably well (in both his social studies and science texts). He also actively participates in discussions about text material.

Question #1: Based upon the limited information presented, what would you conclude about Jack's world knowledge/schemata ? (i.e., is it adequate or inadequate?) Explain your answer.

Question #2: Do you believe that Jack is engaging in more top-down or more bottom-up processing as he reads his content area textbooks? Explain your answer.

Question #3; Is Jack's word identification/decoding accuracy a strength (+) or a weakness (−)? Explain your answer.

Question #4: Is Jack's word identification/decoding automaticity a strength (+) or a weakness (−)? Explain your answer.

Question #5: Is Jack experiencing a trade off of attention as he attempts to read his content area textbooks? Explain your answer.

Question #6: When Jack is called upon to read out loud from his content area texts, is his reading fluent? Explain your answer.

Question #7: Jack's comprehension of his content area texts is reasonably good. Do you think that his comprehension would be even better if someone were to read the text(s) to him? Explain your answer.

3. Frank is a first-grade student. It is the seventh month of the school year and his teacher's observations lead her to conclude that Frank is not off to a good start in learning to read. His teacher believes that it is very important to read a quality piece of children's literature (picture/storybooks, different genres) to the class every day. During these read-aloud sessions, Frank oftentimes appears to be looking elsewhere, not really paying attention to the story. When the teacher asks the children to guess what is going to happen next in the book (and she does this frequently), Frank's hand is never up. When she asks Frank to volunteer a guess, he simply smiles and shakes his head to indicate "No." The teacher has also noticed that when she does the pre-reading activities before introducing a basal reader story (i.e., introducing new vocabulary words), Frank rarely seems to know the meanings of the words.

Question #1: Based upon the very limited information presented above, do you think that Frank has adequate/inadequate world knowledge/schemata ? Explain your answer.

Question #2: Why does Frank have such difficulty predicting that which will happen next in the story? Explain your answer.

Question #3: Why do you think Frank is "not off to a good start in learning to read?" Explain your answer.

REFERENCES

Anderson, Richard. C., & Pearson, P. D. (1984). "A Schema-Theoretic View of Basic Processes in Reading Comprehension." In P. David Pearson, Rebecca Barr, Michael L. Kamil, & Peter Mosenthal (Eds.), *Handbook of Reading Research* (pp. 225–253). New York: Longman.

Brown, D.P. (1954). *Auding as the Primary Language Ability.* Unpublished doctoral dissertation, Stanford University.

Cooper, J. D. (1993). "Understanding Literacy Learning and Constructing Meaning." In *Literacy-Helping Children Construct Meaning* (2nd ed.). Boston/Toronto: Houghton-Mifflin.

Gibson, E.J. & Levin, H. (1975). *The Psychology of Reading.* Cambridge, MA: MIT Press.

Smith, Frank (1994). *Understanding Reading* (5th ed.) Hillsdale, NJ: Lawrence Erlbaum Assoc., Inc.

CHAPTER 6

Listening Comprehension

Key Words/Terms

listening comprehension, auding, linguistic competence, linguistic performance, self-monitoring, reading comprehension potential, oracy, mediating style, text to text connections, text to self connections, text to world connections, interactive episodes of oral reading, unable/unwilling differentiation, affective domain, cognitive domain, regressing, executive control, procedural display, explicit causation, inferred causation, primary causation, secondary causation

Listening comprehension may be defined as an individual's ability to comprehend material that is read to him/her. To differentiate listening comprehension from simply *listening* (i.e., hearing spoken sounds), Brown (1954) coined the term *auding;* he defined auding as the process of listening to language and actively processing it in order to achieve comprehension.

There is general agreement amongst linguists (Menyuk, 1977) that as children "learn to be literate" their *linguistic competence* (i.e., internalized knowledge of language) including listening comprehension skills/strategies, usually exceeds their *linguistic performance* (i.e., ability to use one's internalized knowledge of language to create spoken utterances). Indeed, many of us have had the opportunity to witness a baby's apparent understanding of that which we're saying to him/her well in advance of being able to produce language himself/herself. Similarly, it is not unusual for three-, four- and five-year-olds, when being read to by a parent/caretaker (or others) to exhibit fairly sophisticated listening comprehension (auding) skills/strategies as evidenced by their ability to interact/dialogue with the parent about the story content, characters, setting etc. This ability to actively process (i.e., comprehend) text that is being read to them clearly precedes their ability to comprehend material that they themselves read independently.

It is critically important to understand that listening comprehension and reading comprehension involve very similar processes: In order for an individual to comprehend that which he/she has read, the majority of the words in the text must be part of the reader's receptive vocabulary. Similarly, in order for an individual to comprehend text that has been read to him/her, a majority of the words must be part of the listener's receptive vocabulary. In order for an individual to comprehend that which he/she has read, the reader must sustain attention and concentration; the same is true while listening to material being read. Reading comprehension requires the reader to constantly self-monitor (i.e., self-assess/evaluate) his/her state of comprehension or lack thereof; listening comprehension has the same requirement. Reading comprehension requires active processing (i.e.,metacomprehension) strategies (see chapter 7 for further discussion of metacognition/metacomprehension); listening comprehension requires the same. While attempting to accurately reconstruct the author's intended message, the reader must relate the new information (i.e., textual information) to his/her existing schemata (i.e., new to known); the listener must do the same. In order to comprehend written discourse, the reader must be able to engage in accurate and automatic decoding/word identification ; clearly, *this is not true for listening!* Indeed, simply stated, the most significant difference between reading comprehension and listening comprehension processes is the word identification/decoding variable.

As we human beings emerge into literacy, we first, naturally, learn auding (listening comprehension) skills/strategies; later, as we begin to learn how to read, these same skills/strategies (with the exception of decoding) that we learned during the auding stage are *available* to be transferred to the reading situation. (Note: It is important to stress the word available in the previous sentence; simply because they are available to the reader doesn't necessarily mean that the he/she is going to instantiate (i.e., put to use) these strategies (Cooper, 1993).)

Several researchers have investigated the relationship between listening comprehension (auding ability) and later reading comprehension. Research findings (Loban, 1964) suggest that the former is an excellent predictor of the latter (i.e., listening comprehension is a valid indicator of reading comprehension potential).

In light of the aforementioned, one can see how critically important it is to assess an individual's listening comprehension as part of an overall reading/literacy assessment. Listening comprehension, as has been stated above, has been found to be a reasonably accurate predictor of later reading comprehension.

Similar to the point made in previous chapters re: naturalistic/classroom based assessment, there are numerous opportunities for a teacher to assess his/her students' listening comprehension as the students engage in authentic literacy activities in the classroom. As we know, teachers who understand literacy acquisition and development, are well aware of the fact that reading to their students (regardless of age/grade) on a regular basis is one of the best ways to facilitate their literacy, and perhaps as importantly, foster a lifelong love of books (Trelease, 1989). As teachers read a picture/word book or chapter book to their class, they oftentimes stop periodically to interact with the students about the text.

The teacher who is reading the text aloud to his/her students is, in effect, a mediating agent between the text and the audience. Teachers and parents/caretakers appear to have different mediating styles as they read aloud to children (Voorhees, 1998): Some stop often and ask the listeners questions about the text; some wait until after the entire text/chapter has been read aloud before engaging in questioning behaviors; some ask the class to predict that which is going to happen next; some may ask about the meaning of a particularly challenging vocabulary word in the text; some may ask the students to relate that which has been read to them to other books (i.e., text to text connections); some may ask the students to relate the text to their own lives or the lives of others (text to self/text to world connections); some may point to a word in the book and ask the young readers if anyone can read that word; and some may use other, none, all, or a combination of these interaction techniques.

When teachers enter into any kind of dialogue with their students about a text that has been read to them (NOTE: it must be stressed that we are talking about the teacher reading aloud to the students—NOT the students engaging in oral reading!) the teacher and students are engaging in interactive episodes of oral reading: The teacher is doing the read aloud and the students are listening (i.e., engaging in listening comprehension—assuming that they are at least making some attempt to actively comprehend the text). These teacher student interactions during episodes of oral reading are excellent opportunities for the teacher to informally assess each student's listening comprehension ability.

Clearly, in order to engage in this kind of informal assessment of students' listening comprehension, the teacher must:

1. have an in-depth understanding of comprehension assessment techniques (e.g., retelling, levels of comprehension questions (Herber, 1978);

2. know the approximate level of the texts that are being read to the class;

3. be willing to keep anecdotal evidence of students' performance over time for these interactive read-aloud sessions;

4. know his/her students well in order to differentiate between those instances when a student simply chooses not to respond to a question or participate in a discussion of a text that has been read aloud to the class by the teacher (i.e., unwilling) from those occasions when a student doesn't know the answer to a specific question posed by the teacher or simply doesn't understand the text being discussed and hence is a non-participant in the discussion of the text (i.e., unable). This unwilling/unable differentiation is critical to all informal assessment of student behavior/performance; in most cases, when a student is able but unwilling,, the problem is one involving the affective domain (e.g., attitude, self-concept, confidence level) Conversely, when a student is willing but unable , the problem is most likely caused by a specific skill/strategy/cognitive deficiency; hence, this would involve the cognitive domain).

Figure 6-1. Simple Reading Assessment Model (S-Ram).

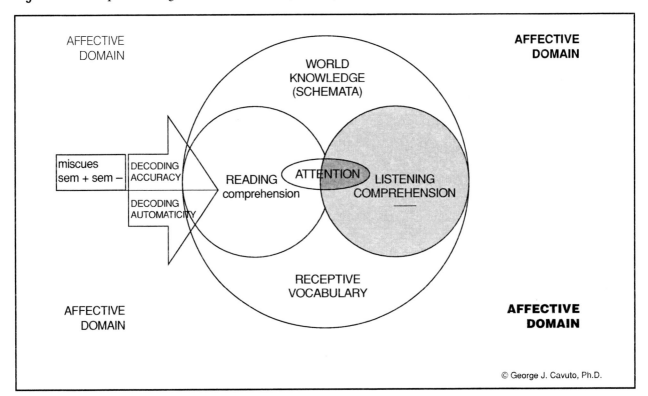

If, after using some of the aforementioned observational techniques, you decide that a particular student in your class has inadequate listening comprehension (i.e., has difficulty answering questions/participating in a dialogue/discussion of Grade Level text that has been read to the class *or* a lecture delivered by the teacher), you should place a minus (–) sign in the listening comprehension section of this student's Simple Reading Assessment Model (S-RAM) [see Figure 6-1].

Conversely, if your observations of this particular student's listening comprehension (over a period of time) appear to indicate that he/she has adequate listening comprehension (i.e., is able to answer questions and/or participate in a dialogue/discussion of GRADE LEVEL text that has been read aloud to the class OR a lecture delivered by the teacher), you should place a (+) sign in the listening comprehension section of this student's Simple Reading Assessment Model (S-RAM) [see Figure 6-2].

Why, one might ask, would a student have inadequate (i.e., below grade level) listening comprehension? There are several possible reasons:

- He/she may have inadequate receptive vocabulary ; if the student doesn't know the meaning of many of the words in the text that is being read aloud by the teacher (or in the lecture that is being delivered by the teacher), it becomes very difficult to understand the text/lecture;

Figure 6-2. Simple Reading Assessment Model (S-Ram).

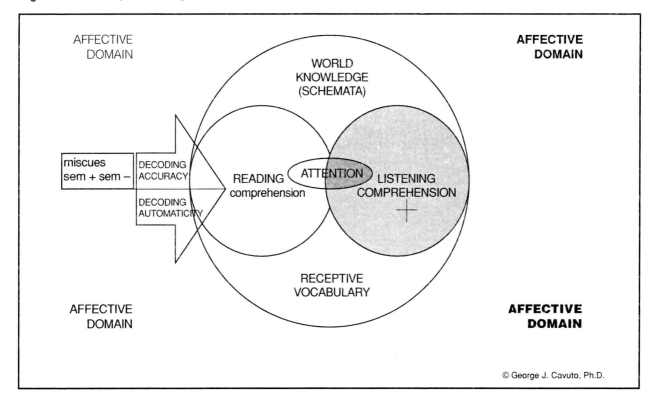

- He/she may have inadequate world knowledge; if the student is unable to relate the material being read to the class by the teacher (new information) (or in the lecture that is being delivered by the teacher), comprehending the meaning will be very difficult/impossible;

- He/she may have difficulty sustaining attention/concentration as the text is being read aloud to the class or as the teacher is delivering a lecture. When text is being read aloud to students by the teacher (or when the teacher is delivering a lecture to the class), in order to engage in auding (i.e., active listening comprehension/processing) of the text or lecture, the listener(s) must be able to sustain attention/concentration. Listening comprehension requires even more sustained attention/concentration than does reading comprehension: While reading, if the reader realizes that he/she has not understood a sentence, paragraph, or series of paragraphs, he/she has the luxury of regressing and re-reading the material to try to fix the breakdown in comprehension. This is sometimes referred to as *executive control* (Brown, 1977): the reader is able to self-monitor his/her state of comprehension and proceed accordingly (e.g., continue reading because the text has been understood, regress and re-read because the text has not been understood, continue reading because the text has not been understood and the reader believes that by continuing on he/she may be able to clear up the confusion/lack of comprehension).

Each of the aforementioned strategies is available to readers because written text is static (i.e., permanent). (Note: Once again, this is *not* to suggest that all readers use these strategies; clearly, some do not!) Conversely, when a student is listening to text being read aloud by the teacher (or listening to the teacher delivering a lecture) and he/she realizes that the information is not making sense/not "sinking in," he/she doesn't have the luxury of re-reading in order to search for the cause of the breakdown and then attempt to "fix-up"; auditory messages, unlike written messages, are not permanent—they are fleeting/ephemeral. Ostensibly, the listener who realizes that his/her comprehension has broken down could interrupt the read aloud (or lecture) and ask the teacher to read a part of the text again (or repeat that portion of the lecture); however, this kind of behavior violates the accepted, unwritten protocol/convention as to how read-aloud and lecture sessions are conducted in classrooms. Without being directly taught this protocol/convention, students inductively learn early on that this behavior (i.e., interrupting the teacher in order to ask him/her to read a part of the text again or repeat a portion of the lecture because there has been a "comprehension breakdown") is unacceptable/undesirable behavior for many reasons: "What would the other students say? Would it be fair to them for me to interrupt the reading? How would the teacher respond to such a request? The other students seem to be 'getting it,' why should I interrupt the teacher simply because I'm not; I don't want to appear 'stupid' to the teacher and/or to my classmates/peers").

In light of the above, as a student is attempting to comprehend text that is being read aloud to the class by the teacher (or a lecture delivered by the teacher), *if* he/she self-monitors and realizes that he/she is no longer understanding the text/lecture (i.e., listening comprehension has broken down), he/she has very limited choices of action:

1. he/she could decide to keep on listening and hope that it begins to make sense;

2. he/she could decide that since it's not making sense anyway, there's no point in continuing to try to listen actively (i.e., aud), so he/she may simply stop attending and allow his/her mind to go elsewhere.

To summarize, inadequate word knowledge (receptive vocabulary), inadequate world knowledge (schemata), and an inability to sustain attention/concentration are explicit (i.e., unambiguous; nothing left to inference) causes of inadequate listening comprehension. Unfortunately, it becomes very "tempting" to suggest that whenever students do not understand material (i.e., age/grade appropriate material) that has been read to them, that they simply were not "paying attention." Tempting, yes; viable, no! As has been stated previously in this section, inadequate word or world knowledge will invariably result in inadequate listening comprehension *regardless* of the listener's ability/inability to sustain attention/concentration. A student could be attending intently to that which is being read to him/her; however, if he/she doesn't know a significant number of word meanings (receptive vocabulary) and/or he/she has insufficient background knowledge (world knowledge, schemata) in order to make text to world and text to self connections, his/her listening comprehension will be inadequate. Simply stated, adequate ability to sustain attention/concentration does not guarantee adequate listening comprehension. However, inadequate ability to sustain attention/concentration as text is being read aloud to the class by the teacher (or as the teacher lectures on any given topic) will *most certainly* result in inadequate listening comprehension.

There is another possible cause for inadequate listening comprehension: the student may be "listening" (i.e., hearing spoken sounds) to that which the teacher is reading aloud to the class or lecturing about; he/she may have adequate word and world knowledge vis-à-vis the text/lecture material; and he/she may be attending/concentrating; however, he/she may not be listening actively (i.e., using metacomprehension strategies). Simply stated, he/she may be a "passive listener." I refer to this as *inferred causation* for the breakdown in listening comprehension.

When there is explicit causation for inadequate listening comprehension (e.g., inadequate word/world knowledge , inability to sustain attention/concentration), this doesn't obviate the possibility that the student is ALSO not engaging in active processing strategies. This may very well be true; however, explicit causation,as the term suggests, does not require any assumptions whatsoever about what the listener may or may not be doing as he/she is listening to text being read aloud; the process *will lack fruition* for very explicit reasons (e.g., inadequate word/world knowledge). Indeed, in some cases there may be both explicit and inferred causation for listening comprehension difficulties. It is important, in terms of an overall assessment of a student's literacy skills/strategies, for the teacher to establish causation for listening comprehension difficulties. Once the causation has been established, appropriate instructional interventions can be planned and implemented. In some cases, the causation for these difficulties will be explicit; in some cases, it/they will be inferred; and in some cases, the causation may be a combination of explicit and inferred.

FOLLOW-UP EXERCISES

Directions: Read the following scenarios and answer the questions that follow.

1. Felix is in the tenth grade. His English teacher, through ongoing, informal observations of Felix's performance in class, has made the following assessments:

    -   Felix appears to have adequate ability to decode material that is age/grade appropriate; his decoding is usually fast and fluent; however, after he finishes reading, his comprehension of the text is often inadequate.

    -   Felix's comprehension doesn't improve when material is read to the class;

    -   Felix appears to have some rather significant gaps in his background knowledge.

    Question #1: Based upon this limited information, would you put a plus (+) or a minus (−) in the listening comprehension section of Felix's Simple Reading Assessment Model (S-RAM)? Explain your answer.

    Question #2: Is word identification/decoding accuracy a strength or a weakness for Felix? Is word identification/decoding automaticity a strength or a weakness? Explain your answers.

    Question #3: Even though Felix's teacher doesn't specifically comment on this, what would you conclude about Felix's receptive vocabulary? Explain your answer.

Question #4: What do you believe is the primary causation for Felix' inadequate listening comprehension? Is the causation explicit or inferred ? Explain your answers.

Question #5: Why does Felix have such poor reading comprehension? Explain your answer.

Question #6: Is Felix experiencing a trade off of attention as he reads text? Explain your answer.

Question #7: Is it possible that there is both explicit and inferred causation for Felix's listening comprehension and reading comprehension difficulties? Explain your answer. If so, which is primary causation and which is secondary causation? Explain your answer.

2. Linda, a third-grade student, is performing "reasonably well" in school (she received all A's and B's on her last report card); however, her parents are concerned because it takes her such a long time to complete her homework (it takes her approximately twice as long as many of her classmates). Linda's teacher and her parents notice the following about her:

    - she is able to figure out almost any word that she comes across in print;

    - she spends a lot of time sounding out the words in her science and social studies texts;

    - her oral reading is not fluent;

    - Linda has excellent comprehension following silent reading of her content area texts; she also has excellent comprehension of text read aloud to the class by the teacher or when text is read aloud to her by her parents;

    - Linda frequently asks her parents to read some of the content area reading assignments to her. Her parents often agree to do so; however, they are not sure if they are helping or hurting by doing this.

Question #1: Is listening comprehension a strength (+) or a weakness (–) for Linda? Explain your answer.

Question #2: Is reading comprehension a strength (+) or a weakness (–) for Linda? Explain your answer.

Question #3: Is Linda experiencing a trade off of attention when she reads? Explain your answer.

Question #4: Although neither her teacher nor her parents specifically commented about her world knowledge (schemata), would you reasonably conclude, based upon the information provided, that this is an area of strength (+) or weakness (–) for Linda? Explain your answer.

Question #5: Although not directly addressed in the above scenario, do you believe that receptive vocabulary is a strength (+) or a weakness (–) for Linda? Explain your answer.

Question #6: Is word identification/decoding accuracy a strength (+) or a weakness (–) for Linda? Explain your answer.

Question #7: Is word identification/decoding automaticity a strength (+) or a weakness (-) for Linda? Explain your answer.

Question #8: Why does Linda prefer that her parents read her content area texts aloud to her rather than reading them silently herself? Explain your answer.

Question #9: Does Linda finish her classwork (e.g., reading textbooks, answering questions) quickly or does it take her somewhat longer? Explain your answer.

Question #10: Based upon the aforementioned information, what would you conclude about Linda's ability to sustain attention/concentration ? Is it a strength (+), a weakness (–) , or is there insufficient information provided in order for you to draw a reasonable conclusion? Explain your answer.

Question #11: Do you think that Linda is engaging in a significant amount of recreational reading? (i.e., does she enjoy reading books during her free time)? Explain your answer.

3. Joshua, a fifth-grade student, has significant difficulty comprehending text that is read aloud to the class by the teacher. His teacher has observed that Joshua has adequate (i.e., age/grade appropriate) receptive vocabulary and schemata. She has also observed that Joshua most certainly appears to have the ability to sustain attention/concentration .

Question #1: Based upon this very limited information, do you think that the causation for Joshua's poor listening comprehension is explicit or inferred ? Explain your answer.

Question #2: What are the causal factors that are negatively impacting on Joshua's listening comprehension? Explain your answer.

Question #3: Based upon the the aforementioned information, what (if anything) could you conclude about Joshua's reading comprehension? Explain your answer.

Question #4: Based upon this very limited information, what could you conclude (if anything) about Joshua's word identification/decoding accuracy? What could you conclude (if anything) about his word identification/decoding automaticity? Explain your answer.

4. If a student has poor listening comprehension, does that necessarily mean that he/she will have poor reading comprehension? Explain your answer. Does it necessarily mean that he/she will have less than adequate receptive vocabulary and schemata? Explain your answer.

REFERENCES

Brown, A.L. (1977). "Knowing when, where and how to remember: A problem of metacognition" (Technical Report No. 47). Urbana: University of Illinois, Center for the Study of Reading.

Brown, D.P. (1954). "Auding as the primary language ability." Unpublished doctoral dissertation, Stanford University.

Cooper, J.D. (1993). "Understanding Literacy Learning and Constructing Meaning." In *Literacy-Helping Children Construct Meaning* (2nd ed.). Boston/Toronto: Houghton-Mifflin.

Herber, H.L. (1978). *Teaching Reading in the Content Areas* (2nd ed.). Englewood Cliffs, NJ: Prentice-Hall.

Loban, W. (1994). "Language ability: Grades seven, eight and nine" (Project No. 1131). University of California, Berkeley.

Menyuk, P. (1977). *Language and Maturation.* Cambridge, MA: MIT Press.

Trelease, J. (1989). *The New Read Aloud Handbook.* New York: Penguin.

Voorhees, S. (1998). *Children's Re-enactments and Parents' Mediating Styles.* Unpublished doctoral dissertation, Hofstra University.

CHAPTER 7

Reading Comprehension

Key Words/Terms

rauding, instantiates schema, literal comprehension, interpretive comprehension, applied comprehension, primary causal factor, secondary causal factor, active processing strategies, metacognitive awareness/metacomprehension strategies, passive reading, self-monitoring, fix-up strategies, mental imaging, self-questioning, relating new to known, passive reading, affective domain, explicit causation, inferred causation

Reading comprehension is an interactive process whereby the reader attempts to accurately reconstruct, through a combination of both bottom-up and top-down processing strategies, the author's intended meaning. In 1977, Carver introduced the term *rauding* to ". . . refer to the receptive communication skills of reading with comprehension and to draw a parallel to the skills of listening with comprehension, or auding (Harris and Hodges, 1995). At any given moment of reading, the reader has two sources of information available:

1. the visual information (textual information) on the page; and

2. the topic specific background knowledge (schema) in his/her head which relates, in some way, to the topic of the textual information.

Clearly, the more background knowledge the reader has to bring to the text, the less he/she has to rely on the textual information (assuming that he/she instantiates/uses this background knowledge). Conversely, the less background knowledge the reader has to bring to the text, the more he/she has to rely on the textual information (Smith, 1994) [See Reading Principle #1, chapter 1]. For this reason, generally speaking, readers who have a well-developed schemata are predisposed to being better reading comprehenders than readers who have a paucity of background knowledge to bring to the page.

As was mentioned in the previous chapter dealing with listening comprehension , there are several reasons why a listener may not understand text that is being read to him/her. These reasons for breakdowns in listening comprehension were referred to as causal factors; they were divided into two types: explicit causation and inferred causation. Moreover, a differentiation was also made between primary causation and secondary causation. These concepts apply in *exactly the same way* to the process of reading comprehension. When assessing an individual's reading comprehension, it is critically important to ascertain whether his/her reading comprehension is adequate/inadequate after reading grade level text; and the reason(s) for inadequate reading comprehension.

There are numerous opportunities for a teacher to naturalistically/informally assess his/her students' reading comprehension in the classroom: If the class is reading a piece of literature (or if the class is divided into literature discussion groups), a student's ability to answer specific, teacher directed questions about the novel, short story, play, poem, etc. is usually an excellent indicator of his/her reading comprehension or lack thereof. Similarly, students' ability to comprehend their content area texts (e.g., social studies, science) is also an excellent indicator of reading comprehension.

Much like the points made earlier in this text regarding detecting patterns of behavior over time, as opposed to one moment in time assessments, it is very important for the teacher to be aware of the types of reading comprehension questions with which a particular student may be having difficulty; keeping anecdotal notes is very helpful in this regard. Herber (1978) suggests three levels of reading/listening comprehension: literal, interpretive, and applied. Very simply stated, a comprehension question is literal if the answer to it can be found on the lines, a comprehension question is interpretive if its answer is found between the lines, and the comprehension question is applied if the answer to it is found beyond the lines.

Literal comprehension questions require the student to process text at a factual level; this requires very little, if any, real understanding of the text. Literal comprehension questions can be answered by the student simply retrieving factual information from the text.

Example: "The preplanning synergism is part of the linguistic performance system." Q: "What is the preplanning synergism?" A: "It is part of the linguistic performance system."

Interpretive comprehension questions, on the other hand, require the reader to process text at a deeper level. When, for example, the reader is asked to make an inference (i.e., draw a conclusion), ascertain a main idea or thesis, detect the author's tone, he/she is being asked an interpretive level question. *Applied comprehension* questions, the most difficult type of comprehension questions, require the reader to use a significant amount of *text extrinsic information* (Herber, 1978) (i.e., beyond the lines information) in order to formulate a reasonable response.

Example: Q: "In chapter 1 of Steinbeck's *Of Mice and Men,* we see a very interesting relationship developing between George and Lenny. Describe this relationship and discuss at least one other novel that you have read where the characters appear to have a similar kind of relationship."

Answers to literal comprehension questions and interpretive comprehension questions may involve a single word or phrase; however, answers to applied comprehension questions are almost always significantly more lengthy. Herber also makes the excellent point that each level of comprehension is a prerequisite for the next higher level (i.e., if a student is unable to process text at a factual/literal level, he/she will most likely not be able to process text at an interpretive or applied level).

If, after using some of the aforementioned observational techniques, you decide that a particular student in your class *consistently* has inadequate reading comprehension (after reading grade level text), you should place a minus (–) sign in the reading comprehension section of the Simple Reading Assessment Model (S-RAM) [see Figure 7-1].

Conversely, if your ongoing observations over time clearly indicate that a student in your class has adequate reading comprehension, (after reading grade level text), you should place a plus (+) sign in the reading comprehension section of the Simple Reading Assessment Model (S-RAM) [see Figure 7-2].

Assessing that a particular student in your class has inadequate reading comprehension is the first, and perhaps most critical, step toward developing an intervention/instructional program for this youngster. However, as you become more and more proficient at classroom based/naturalistic assessment of your students' reading behaviors/strategies, you should strive to be even more specific re: each student's specific reading comprehension strengths and weaknesses. The reading comprehension section of the Simple Reading Assessment Model (S-RAM) may be subdivided into three sections reflecting the three levels of reading comprehension: literal , interpretive , and applied [see Figure 7-3].

Teachers may wish to fine-tune their assessments of students with reading comprehension difficulties by placing plus (+) or minus (–) signs in *each of the three sections* to represent a particular student's ability to deal with *each level of reading comprehension.* [Note: It is *not* necessary to do this for students who the teacher has assessed as having adequate reading comprehension of grade level texts; this assessment implies that the student is able to *consistently* comprehend text at each of these levels.]

Figure 7-1. Simple Reading Assessment Model (S-Ram).

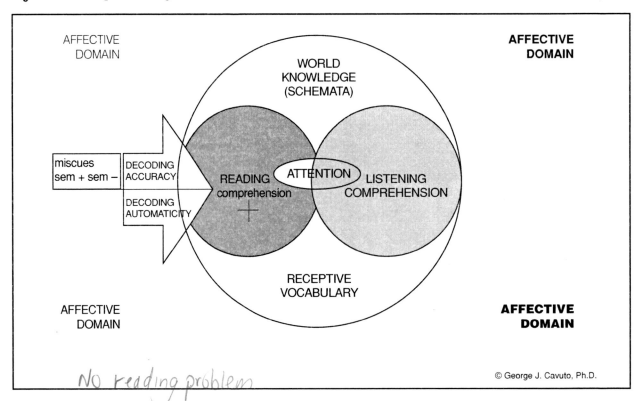

reading problem

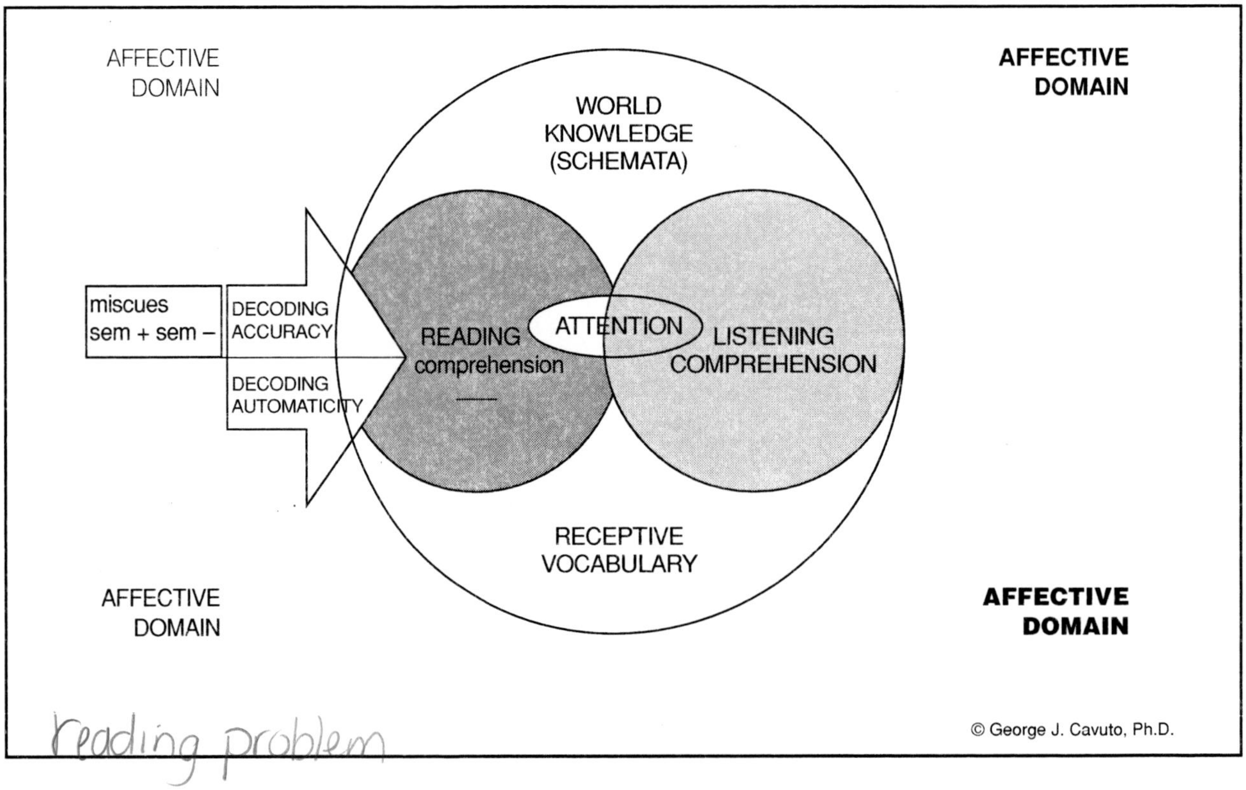

Figure 7-2. Simple Reading Assessment Model (S-Ram).

Figure 7-3. Simple Reading Assessment Model (S-Ram).

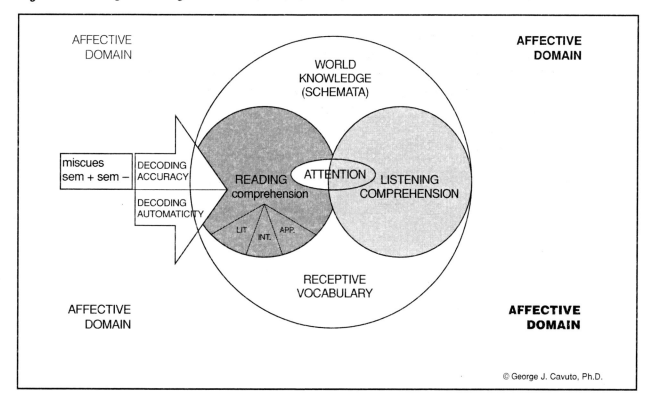

Once it has been established that a student has inadequate reading comprehension (in one, two, or three levels of reading comprehension), it becomes important to ascertain the reason(s) for this deficiency. There are several reasons (i.e.,causal factors) why students may experience reading comprehension difficulties; they include the following.

Inadequate Word Identification/Decoding Accuracy

If a student attempts to read grade level text and encounters a *significant* amount of difficulty (i.e., more than 10 percent of the words are decoded incorrectly [counting semantically acceptable miscues as correct]) breaking the code (i.e., word recognition accuracy), there can be little doubt that his/her comprehension of that text will be inadequate. Insufficient/inadequate word recognition accuracy is oftentimes a primary explicit causal factor re: inadequate reading comprehension. Primary explicit causation is indicated on the Simple Reading Assessment Model (S-RAM) with a large, solid arrow. [See Figure 7-4.]

Note: The word *explicit* is used when the causation for the reading comprehension inadequacy, either primary or secondary, is one of the other sections of the S-RAM MODEL. When the causation, either primary or secondary, is *not* one of the other sections of the S-RAM MODEL, I refer to this as *inferred causation.*

Figure 7-4. Simple Reading Assessment Model (S-Ram).

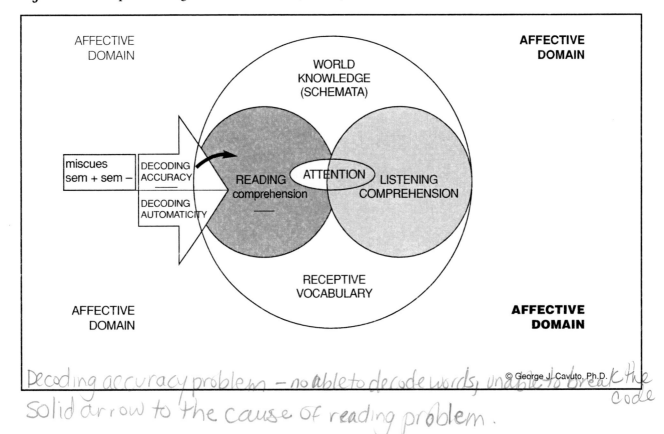

Decoding accuracy problem — no able to decode words, unable to break the code solid arrow to the cause of reading problem.

Inadequate Word Identification/Decoding Automaticity

If a student attempts to read grade level text and correctly decodes *most* of the words (i.e., has more than 90 percent word recognition/decoding accuracy (counting semantically acceptable miscues as correct), but has to mediate many (i.e., more than 30 percent) of the words, he/she may have poor reading comprehension due to a trade off of attention (see chapter 2). Insufficient/inadequate word identification/decoding automaticity is sometimes a primary explicit causal factor inadequate reading regarding comprehension. (See Figure 7-5.)

It has been my experience that inadequate word identification/decoding automaticity is MORE OFTEN a secondary explicit causal factor influencing a student's reading comprehension. If a student is experiencing BOTH inadequate word identification/decoding accuracy AND inadequate word identification/decoding automaticity, I would consider the word identification/decoding accuracy the primary explicit causal factor for the reading comprehension inadequacy; the inadequate word identification/decoding automaticity is considered a secondary explicit causal factor. [Note: Secondary explicit causation is indicated on the Simple Reading Assessment Model (S-RAM) with a smaller, hollow arrow. (See Figure 7-6.)]

Figure 7-5. Simple Reading Assessment Model (S-Ram).

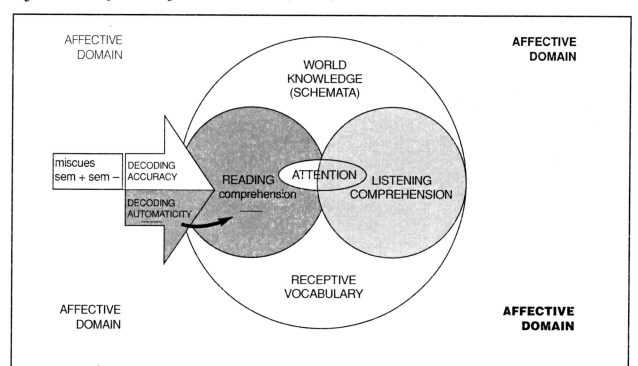

Figure 7-6. Simple Reading Assessment Model (S-Ram).

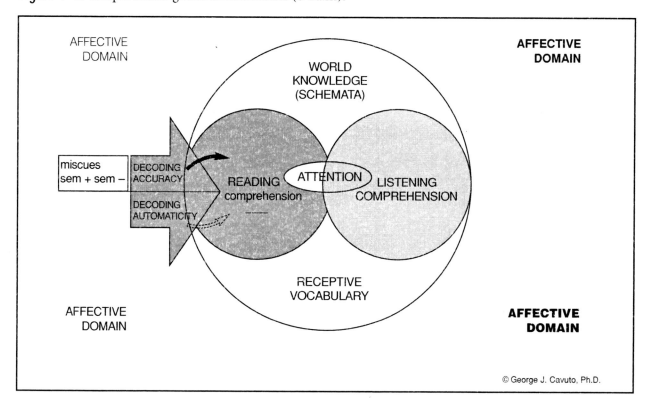

Figure 7-7. Simple Reading Assessment Model (S-Ram).

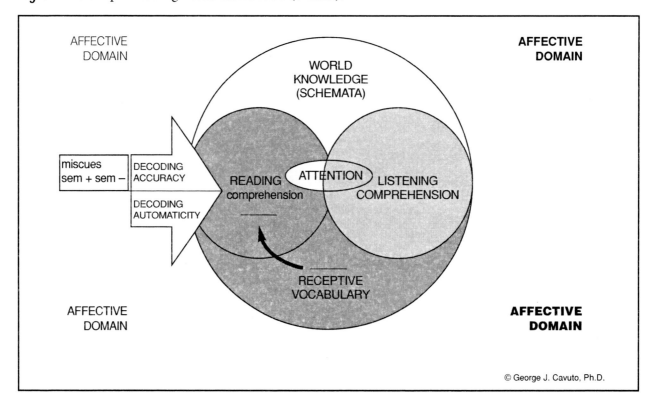

© George J. Cavuto, Ph.D.

Inadequate Receptive Vocabulary

If a student attempts to read grade level text and does not know the meaning of a significant number of key words in the text, he/she will most likely have inadequate comprehension of the text. Note: The aforementioned phrase *key words* is very important here. A student can read a page of text and not know the meaning of several of the words; however, if these words are not key (i.e., central) to the main ideas expressed on that page, it is possible that his/her comprehension may be adequate; conversely, if the words that are unfamiliar to the student are key/central to the main idea(s) being expressed on the page, more than likely his/her comprehension of that page of text will be unsatisfactory.] Inadequate receptive vocabulary is oftentimes a primary explicit causation of inadequate reading comprehension. (See Figure 7-7.)

It is important to stress once again (as we did in chapter 6) that the converse is not necessarily true: A student may know the meaning of virtually all of the words on a page of text and yet finish reading that page feeling as if he/she has understood nothing at all!

Inadequate World Knowledge/Schemata

If a student has inadequate background knowledge re: the specific topic being read (i.e., schema), he/she will be predisposed to having inadequate reading comprehension. As was discussed in Chapter One, there is a reciprocal relationship which exists between background knowledge and text information: the more background knowledge (schema) that a reader brings to a particular text, the less that reader has to rely on textual (visual) information; conversely, the less background knowledge (schema) that a reader brings to a particular text, the more that reader has to rely on textual (visual) information (Smith, 1994). When a reader has a reasonable amount of schema to bring to a text, he/she can engage in top-down processing (i.e., making both focal and global predictions) (Smith, 1994); this kind of processing facilitates comprehension; conversely, when a reader has limited or no schema to bring to a text, he/she has to engage in mostly bottom-up (i.e., text-based) processing. Although this does NOT make comprehension impossible, it most certainly makes it more difficult (hence the use of the word predisposed in the first sentence of this paragraph.) Inadequate/insufficient world knowledge to bring to a particular text (schema) is oftentimes a primary explicit causation of inadequate reading comprehension. (See Figure 7-8.)

Inability to Sustain Attention/Concentration

If a youngster is unable to sustain attention/concentration while reading, this will make it very difficult, if not impossible, for him/her to comprehend that which has

Figure 7-8. Simple Reading Assessment Model (S-Ram).

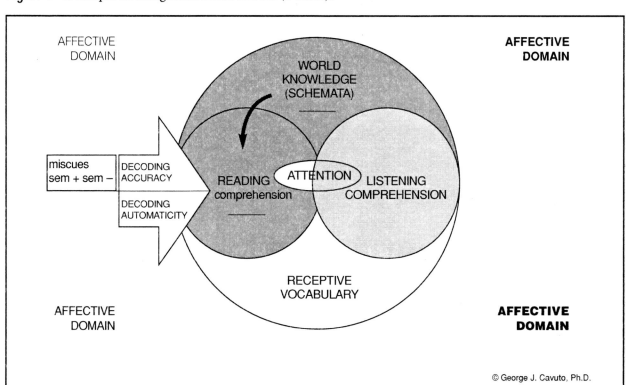

been read. However, it is very important that teachers don't fall into the circuitous reasoning trap of generalizing and blaming all reading comprehension inadequacies on an inability to attend/concentrate.

Example: **Teacher:** Joey has a hard time understanding that which he reads in his social studies, science and language arts texts; he must not be paying attention/concentrating. **Parent:** How can you be sure that he is not attending/concentrating as he reads? **Teacher:** Because he has very poor comprehension!

Clearly, this kind of circuitous reasoning only serves to further confuse the issue; it also doesn't do that which all valid assessment should do—inform instruction!

If a student has *across-the-board* (i.e., in ALL subject areas) difficulty sustaining attention/concentration, and there are no other explicit or implicit causal factors impacting on his/her reading comprehension, inadequate attention/concentration would then be considered a primary explicit causal factor for his/her inadequate reading comprehension. (See Figure 7-9.)

If, for example, this same student who has across-the-board difficulty sustaining attention/concentration also has severe deficiencies in word recognition/decoding accuracy, I would consider the lack of word identification/decoding

Figure 7-9. Simple Reading Assessment Model (S-Ram).

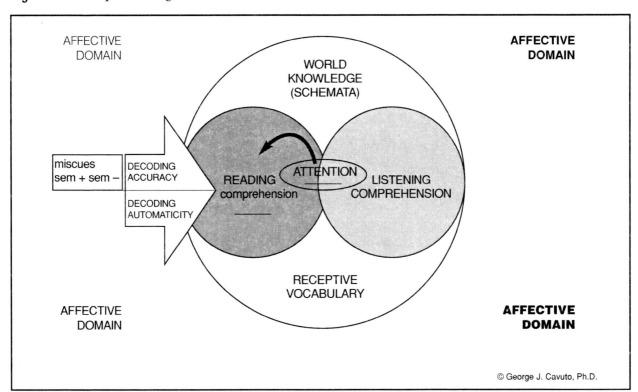

Figure 7-10. Simple Reading Assessment Model (S-Ram).

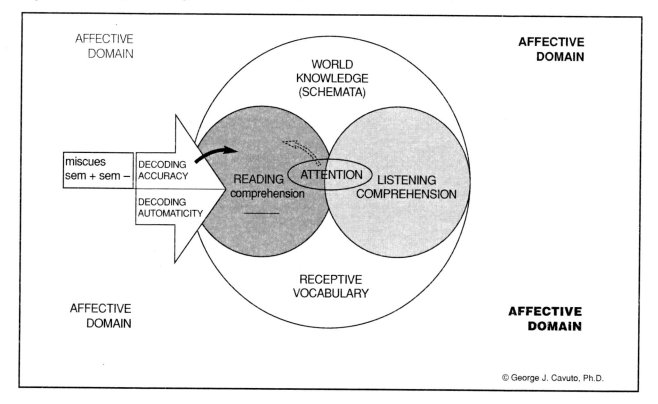

accuracy to be the primary explicit causal factor influencing the poor reading comprehension; I would consider the difficulty sustaining attention/concentration as a secondary, explicit causal factor.

When there are multiple, explicit causal factors negatively impacting on a student's reading comprehension, deciding which are primary and which are secondary is most certainly a judgment call. Making this differentiation is not nearly as important as realizing that there may, in fact, be several reasons (i.e., causal factors) for the inadequate reading comprehension. As a general rule of thumb, when there are multiple causes of a reading comprehension inadequacy, I tend to consider those things that are most amenable to instructional intervention to be primary (e.g., word identification/decoding accuracy, word identification/decoding automaticity, receptive vocabulary, world knowledge) and those things that are not as amenable to instructional intervention to be secondary (e.g., attention/concentration span, affective domain).

Lack of Metacognitive Awareness/Metacomprehension Strategies (Passive Reading)

In order for adequate reading comprehension to occur, the reader MUST engage active processing strategies as he/she attempts to accurately reconstruct the author's intended message. Active readers do several things as they read. They constantly "self-monitor" (ongoing self-assessment of their state of comprehension of the text) themselves by asking, "Does this make sense?" If the answer to this question is, "Yes," they continue reading; if the answer is "No," they re-read the passage/selection using *fix-up strategies;* these strategies include: *mental imaging* (creating mental pictures/images of that which has been read), *self-questioning* (asking Who? What? When? Where? Why? and How? questions about the text that has been read), and *relating new to known* (attempting to relate/analogize the textual information to information that is already part of the reader's schemata).

Interestingly enough, many active readers do not recall ever being directly taught these strategies; they seem to have simply developed them as part of their reading/language processing experiences. *Passive readers,* on the other hand, often have no idea whatsoever that the reader must take a proactive role if a text is to be understood. It is not unusual for passive readers to engage in "word calling" (i.e., simply breaking the written code and assuming that the brain will automatically take care of the rest!). Jago, a secondary school English teacher, makes this point quite well: "Even when students dutifully eyeball the assigned pages, few think the homework assignment has asked them for anything more. Students turn on their stereos, kick back on their beds, and expect the book to transfer information from its pages to their brains." (Jago, 1999/2000, p. 45.)

There are many students who have everything they need (i.e., adequate word recognition/decoding accuracy, adequate word recognition/decoding automaticity, adequate receptive vocabulary, adequate world knowledge/ schemata, and adequate ability to sustain attention/concentration) to be adequate reading comprehenders, yet despite these strengths, they consistently experience significant difficulty comprehending written text. This type of reading comprehension difficulty does not have primary explicit causation. In these cases we must rely on decades of research in the area of metacognition/metacomprehension in order to establish, what we will refer to as *primary inferred causation* (represented by a large, hollow arrow on the S-RAM). For these students, lack of metacognitive awareness/metacomprehension strategies would be considered the primary inferred causation for their reading comprehension difficulties. This type of causation is represented on the S-RAM with a large, hollow arrow going from the metacognitive/metacomprehension strategies (listed in the lower right-hand corner of the model) to the reading comprehension circle. (See Figure 7-11.)

There are also many students for whom lack of metacognitive awareness/metacomprehension strategies is a secondary inferred causation for their reading comprehension difficulties; this would be the case when inadequate word identification/decoding accuracy, inadequate word identification/decoding automaticity, inadequate receptive vocabulary, inadequate world knowledge/ schemata, and/or inadequate attention/concentration is/are primary explicit causation(s) for the inadequate reading comprehension.

Figure 7-11. Simple Reading Assessment Model (S-Ram).

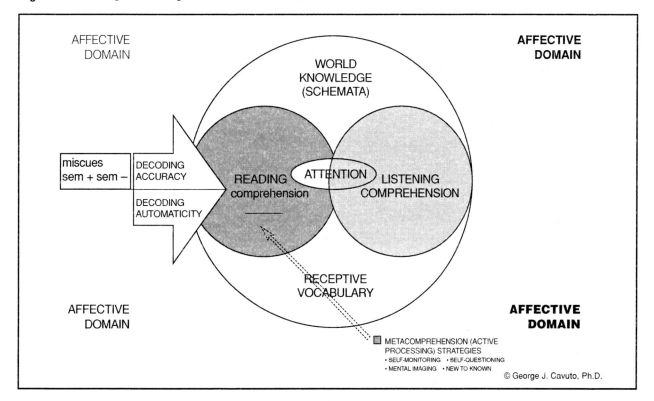

Insufficient Motivation (Affective Domain)

"Without sufficient interest in acquiring knowledge in a given domain, it becomes difficult to attend in a way that optimizes the probability of success in reading" (Vellutino & Denckla, 1991, p. 57). Clearly, if a student lacks sufficient motivation to read and understand a particular text, his/her reading comprehension will more than likely be inadequate. However, one has to be very careful not to attribute causation for inadequate reading comprehension to affective considerations when there are very specific deficiencies (see above) that are causing poor reading comprehension. Indeed, if ANY of the abovementioned causal factors are present, the student MAY very well appear to be lacking in interest/motivation when, in fact, the real problem is actually skill/strategy deficiencies. This point notwithstanding, there are certainly "some" students who have perfectly adequate skills/strategies to bring to text, yet consistently read text with inadequate comprehension due to a lack of interest/motivation. A pattern of this kind of behavior would be considered a problem in the affective domain as the primary inferred causation for the reading comprehension difficulty. (See Figure 7-12.)

Note: The reason that I refer to affective domain causation as *inferred causation* is that judgments made about affective considerations are more often than not inferred rather than explicit; hence the large hollow arrow (rather than a solid arrow) in Figure 7-12.

Figure 7-12. Simple Reading Assessment Model (S-Ram).

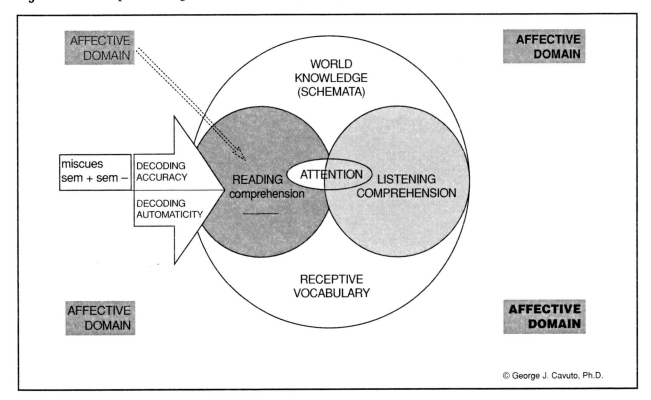

© George J. Cavuto, Ph.D.

As a general rule of thumb, I have found that most students want to do well in school; hence, over the long term, they will make every attempt to read even *neutral material* (i.e., material that they do not find particularly interesting) actively. In my experience, reading comprehension inadequacies rarely have as their primary causation insufficient interest/motivation. I have found that affective concerns (e.g., poor motivation, low self-esteem, lack of self-confidence) are more often a consequence of poor reading comprehension rather than its cause. For this reason, it appears reasonable to suggest that affective considerations are more often a secondary (rather than a primary) inferred causation for reading comprehension difficulties. (See Figure 7-13.)

Once again, a word of caution: before deciding that a lack of interest/motivation is a primary or secondary causal factor influencing a student's inadequate reading comprehension, remember that most of us human beings do not like to do that which we have difficulty doing ; hence, what sometimes appears to be lack of interest/motivation is oftentimes a skill/strategy deficiency.

To summarize, it is critically important that teachers assess the reading comprehension strengths and weaknesses for each of their students at each of three levels of comprehension: the literal level, the interpretive level, and the applied level. If a student has inadequate reading comprehension at one or more of these levels of comprehension when attempting to read grade level text, it is important to establish causation for the breakdown in reading comprehension. It is of lesser

Figure 7-13. Simple Reading Assessment Model (S-Ram).

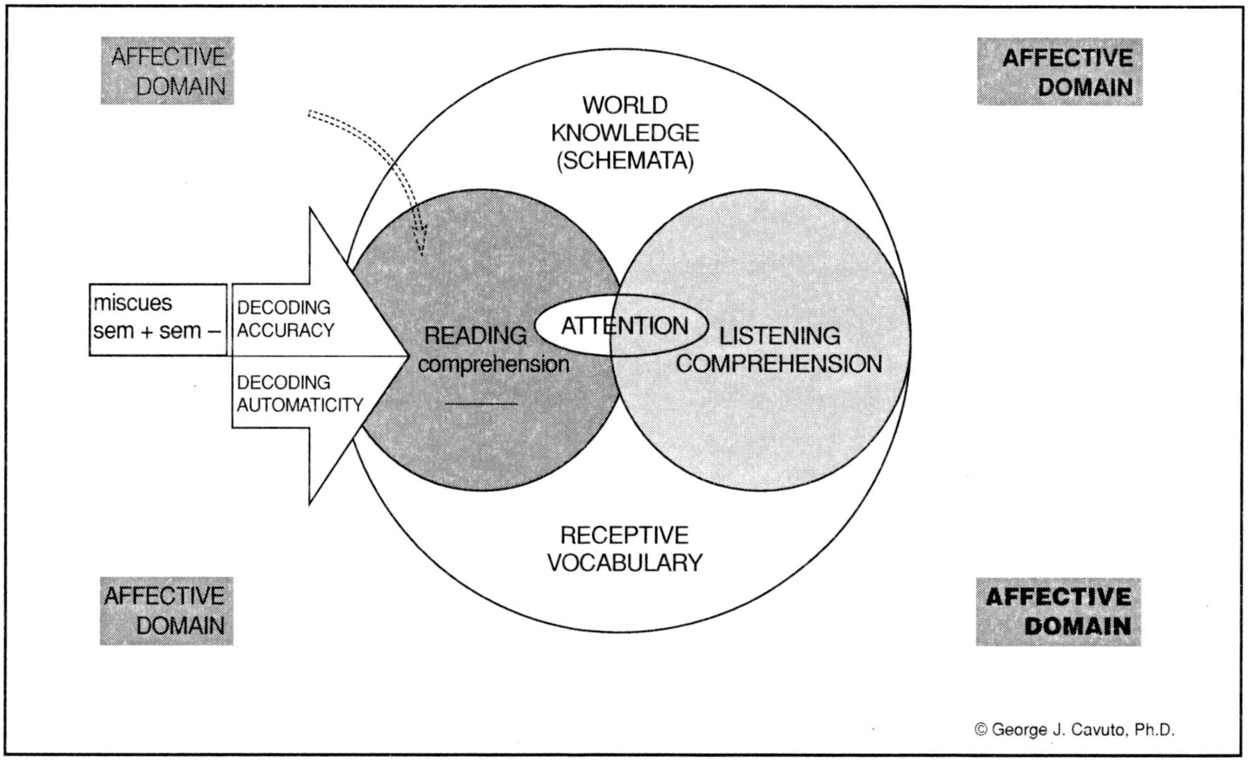

importance, but interesting from a reading assessment as problem-solving perspective, to differentiate between/among primary explicit causation, primary inferred causation, secondary explicit causation, and secondary inferred causation. Only by clearly establishing causation for the reading comprehension difficulty (which is, in MOST cases, students' major area of reading deficiency) can an appropriate instructional/intervention plan be devised.

FOLLOW-UP EXERCISES

1. Joseph is a fourth-grade student. Joseph's teacher has made the following classroom observations:

Joseph appears to have an excellent knowledge of word meanings; he is the first to put up his hand when the class is asked the meaning of a word. He is also very good at decoding words; in fact, I often hear him, in an audible voice, systematically sounding out many of the words as he's reading silently at his seat. Joseph takes much longer than the other students in my class to finish social studies, science, and literature assignments from his textbooks; he also appears to miss the point of that which he has read. During discussions following the reading of these texts, he has little to offer, even when called upon to do so; interestingly enough, Joseph does enjoy when I read a novel to the class and he is an enthusiastic participant in those discussions. Joseph appears to be motivated to do well; however, he is getting C's in three of his major subjects. Thank goodness that his math computational skills are so good. I can give him a math worksheet and he will work nonstop for 45 minutes and achieve a 100 percent score. I really don't know what's going on with him—he's a mystery to me!

Question 1: How would you rate (+ or −) Joseph's receptive vocabulary, or is there not enough information to make a decision? Explain your answer.

+ excellent knowledge of word meanings.
receptive vocabulary isnot impacting reading
ability

Question 2: How would you rate (+ or −) Joseph's world knowledge/schemata, or is there not enough information to make a decision? Explain your answer.

+ good vocabulary
able to have discussions when
read to.

Question 3: How would you rate (+ or −) Joseph's reading comprehension, or is there not enough information to make a decision? Explain your answer.

— misses the point as he reads.

Question 4: How would you rate (+ or −) Joseph's listening comprehension, or is there not enough information to make a decision? Explain your answer.

+ enjoys and takes part in discussions
lots to over in discussions

Question 5: How would you rate (+ or −) Joseph's word recognition/decoding accuracy, or is there not enough information to make a decision? Explain your answer.

+ Very good at decoding

Question 6: How would you rate (+ or −) Joseph's word recognition/decoding automaticity, or is there not enough information to make a decision? Explain your answer.

— sounds out words at seat.

Causal factor - due to automaticity because of trade off of attention

Question 7: Joseph's teacher finds him to be a "mystery." What do you believe is the primary causation for his reading comprehension difficulty? Explain your answer. Are there secondary causations for his reading comprehension difficulty? Explain your answer.

listening comp. helps us better understand
Comprehension piece.
for poor listening comp:
Attention or not actively listening
No background knowledge or vocabulary

2. If a student has inadequate word identification/decoding accuracy and inadequate word knowledge (receptive vocabulary), is it possible that there can be primary inferred causation for his/her inadequate reading comprehension? Explain your answer.

3. Brendan is a third-grade student. Brendan's teacher has made the following notes about his classroom performance: "much difficulty figuring out words; very slow, plodding reader; doesn't like to read; limited knowledge of word meanings; needs to be pushed to pick out a book from the school library." Based on this very limited information, answer the following questions:

Question 1: Do you believe that Brendan has adequate or inadequate reading comprehension, or is there insufficient information presented to make a decision? Explain your answer.

Question 2: What can you conclude about Brendan's receptive vocabulary, or is there insufficient information presented to make a decision? Explain your answer.

Question 3: What can you conclude about Brendan's world knowledge/schemata, or is there insufficient information presented to make a decision? Explain your answer.

Question 4: What can you conclude about Brendan's listening comprehension, or is there insufficient information presented to make a decision? Explain your answer.

Question 5: What are some reasons why Brendan may "need to be pushed" to choose a book from the library?

Question 6: What are the "causal factors" that are impacting on Brendan's major area of reading deficiency? Is the causation explicit or inferred? Explain your answer.

4. Geraldo, a ninth-grade student, has poor reading comprehension, adequate receptive vocabulary and schemata; he also has grade appropriate word identification/decoding accuracy skills; however, his word identification/decoding automaticity is significantly below his grade level placement. Geraldo appears to be "turned off" to reading. When asked about his reading, he usually responds, "Hey, I just don't like to read, it's boring!" Do you believe that the affective domain should be considered a primary explicit causation for Geraldo's reading comprehension weakness? Explain your answer.

5. Beth, a sixth-grade student, has excellent reading comprehension. What can you conclude about her receptive vocabulary? What can you conclude about her world knowledge/schemata? What can you conclude about her word identification/decoding accuracy? What can you conclude about her word identification/decoding automaticity? What can you conclude about her listening comprehension? Explain your answers.

6. Gina, an eighth-grade student, is having considerable difficulty with science, social studies and language arts. Gina is a student who works very hard, sometimes spending two or three hours a night doing her homework. She has excellent background knowledge; she has no difficulty whatsoever figuring out words in her grade-level texts and is able to do so quickly; however, she has always had difficulty in reading comprehension despite apparent satisfactory attention/concentration. Answer the following questions based on the aforementioned information.

Question 1: Is word knowledge a strength (+) or a weakness for Gina, or is there insufficient information presented to made a decision? Explain your answer.

Question 2: Is Gina predisposed to being an adequate reading comprehender? Explain your answer.

Question 3: What do you believe is the primary causation for Gina's reading comprehension difficulty? Is this causation explicit or inferred? Explain your answer.

Question 4: Does there appear to be a secondary causation for Gina's reading comprehension difficulty? Explain your answer.

7. Shane is a fifth-grade student. His teacher has made the following classroom observations:

Shane has some difficulty reading aloud in class; he gets the words correct, however, it takes him quite some time to do so . . . he lacks fluency. When I ask him about the meaning of some of the more technical words in the science and social studies texts, he oftentimes does not know the meanings. Understanding what he reads continues to be a problem area as well: He can usually find the answers to factual questions; however, questions that require a deeper understanding of the text give him considerable difficulty; this is true whether Shane reads the text or someone reads it to him."

Fill in each section of the Simple Reading Assessment Model (S-RAM) below. Draw large, solid arrows to indicate explicit primary causation (i.e., for his reading comprehension difficulty) and smaller, solid arrows to indicate explicit secondary causation for his reading comprehension difficulty. Is there any inferred causation for Shane's major area of reading deficiency? Explain your answer.

Simple Reading Assessment Model (S-Ram).

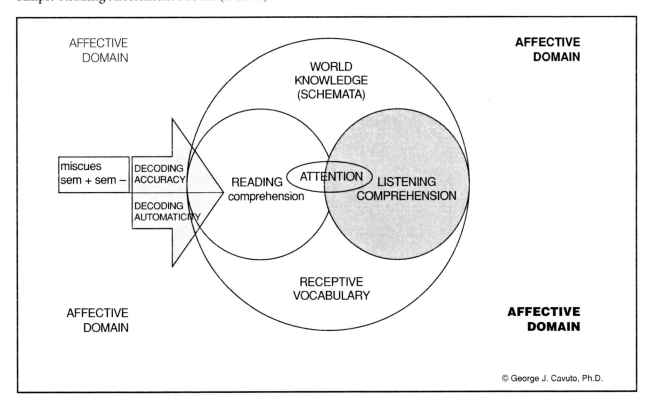

8. Meghan is a sixth-grade student. Her teacher has started to keep an "anecdotal" log of Meghan's literacy performance in class. The last three entries are as follows:

3/14—'industrial,' 'manufacture,' 'commerce,' . . . ["I don't know"] 3/18—didn't know 'sympathetic,' 'boast,' 'demons 3/19—very upset . . . I can't answer these questions Mrs. Clark!

Based upon this very limited information, what would you conclude, if anything, about Meghan's word knowledge? her world knowledge/schemata? her reading comprehension? her listening comprehension? her word identification accuracy? her word identification automaticity? her attention/concentration span? causation? Explain your answers.

REFERENCES

Harris, Theodore L., and Hodges, Richard E. (Eds.) (1995). *The Literacy Dictionary.* Newark, DE: International Reading Association.

Herber, H.L. (1978). *Teaching Reading in the Content Areas* (2nd ed.). Englewood Cliffs, NJ: Prentice-Hall.

Jago, Marilyn. *American Educator* (Winter 99/2000).

Smith, Frank (1994). *Understanding Reading* (5th ed.). Hillsdale, NJ: Lawrence Erlbaum Assoc., Inc.

Vellutino, Frank R., and Denckla, Martha B. (1991). "Cognitive and neuropsychological foundations of word identification in poor and normally developing readers." In Rebecca Barr, Michael l. Kamil, Peter Mosenthal, and P. David Pearson (Eds.), *Handbook of Reading Research: Volume II* (pp. 571–608). New York: Longman.

Using Observations in One Aspect of the Reading Process to Predict Other Aspects of the Process

---

word identification/decoding accuracy, word identification/decoding automaticity, semantically unacceptable miscues, trade off of attention principle, mediated word identification/decoding, bottom-up processing, top-down processing, self-correction, self-monitoring, high graphophonic miscues, deep structure level

When using the Simple Reading Assessment Model (S-RAM), one aspect of the reading process (i.e., one section of the model) may be used to make reasonable predictions (which, of course, must be either corroborated or rejected after much classroom-based observations) about other aspects (i.e., section(s) of the model) of the reading process. The following are reasonable inferences based upon the information given.

1. If a student has a weakness in word identification/decoding accuracy (-WR/D ACC), it can be reasonably inferred that this student will also have a weakness in word identification/decoding automaticity (-WR/D AUT). It would be impossible for a student to be a poor "word identifier/decoder" but yet be able to correctly decode words automatically; this would be an inherent contradiction. In formulaic form:

$$\text{-WR/D ACC} \longrightarrow \text{-WR/D AUT}$$

In S-RAM form: (See Figure 8-1.)

Figure 8-1. Simple Reading Assessment Model (S-Ram).

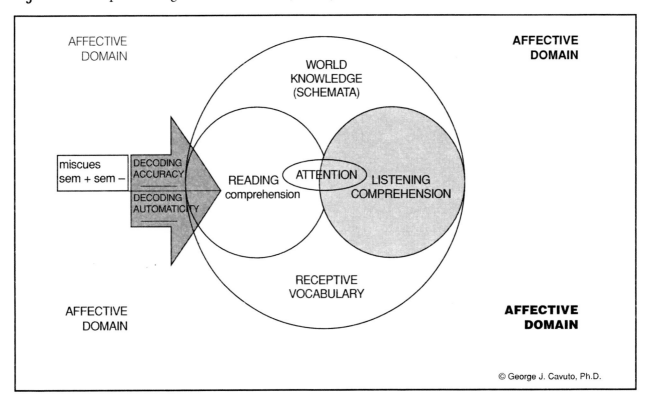

2. If a student has a weakness in word identification/decoding accuracy (-WR/D ACC), it can be reasonably inferred that this student will also have a weakness in reading comprehension (-RC). Clearly, if the student has significant difficulty breaking the code (i.e. identifying words), it would be very difficult/impossible for him/her to comprehend that which he/she has read. This student would most likely make a majority of semantically unacceptable miscues (i.e., miscues that significantly distort the author's intended meaning) and would, in all probability, leave them uncorrected. In formulaic form:

$$\text{-WR/D ACC} \longrightarrow \text{-RC}$$

In S-RAM form: (See Figure 8-2.)

3. If a student has adequate word identification/decoding accuracy (+WR/D ACC) but inadequate word identification/decoding automaticity (-WR/D AUT), one could reasonably predict that this student may have poor reading comprehension due to a trade off of attention (i.e., giving so much attention to the word identification/decoding aspect of reading that there is little attention (cognitive energy) left to devote to meaning).

(Note: There are some students, however, who do a great deal of mediated word identification/decoding and yet have adequate reading

Figure 8-2. Simple Reading Assessment Model (S-Ram).

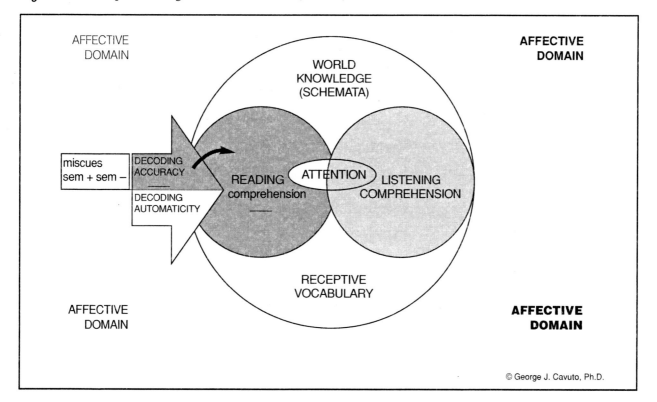

comprehension; for the most part, I have found that these are usually students who have extensive schemata vis-à-vis the text to be read. It seems as though they are able to compensate for much attention being given to bottom-up processing by simply having a large storehouse of topic specific background knowledge (i.e., schema) to aid in their understanding of text.)

In formulaic form:

$$+\text{WR/D ACC and -WR AUT} \longrightarrow \text{-RC}$$

In S-RAM form: (See Figure 8-3.)

4. If a student has inadequate/poor receptive vocabulary (-RV), one could reasonably predict that this student will have poor reading comprehension (-RC) and poor listening comprehension (-LC). It is extremely difficult, if not impossible, to understand that which one reads/listens to if one doesn't know the meaning of the key words in that particular reading selection. In formulaic form:

$$-\text{RV} \longrightarrow \text{-RC and -LC}$$

In S-RAM form: (See Figure 8-4.)

Figure 8-3. Simple Reading Assessment Model (S-Ram).

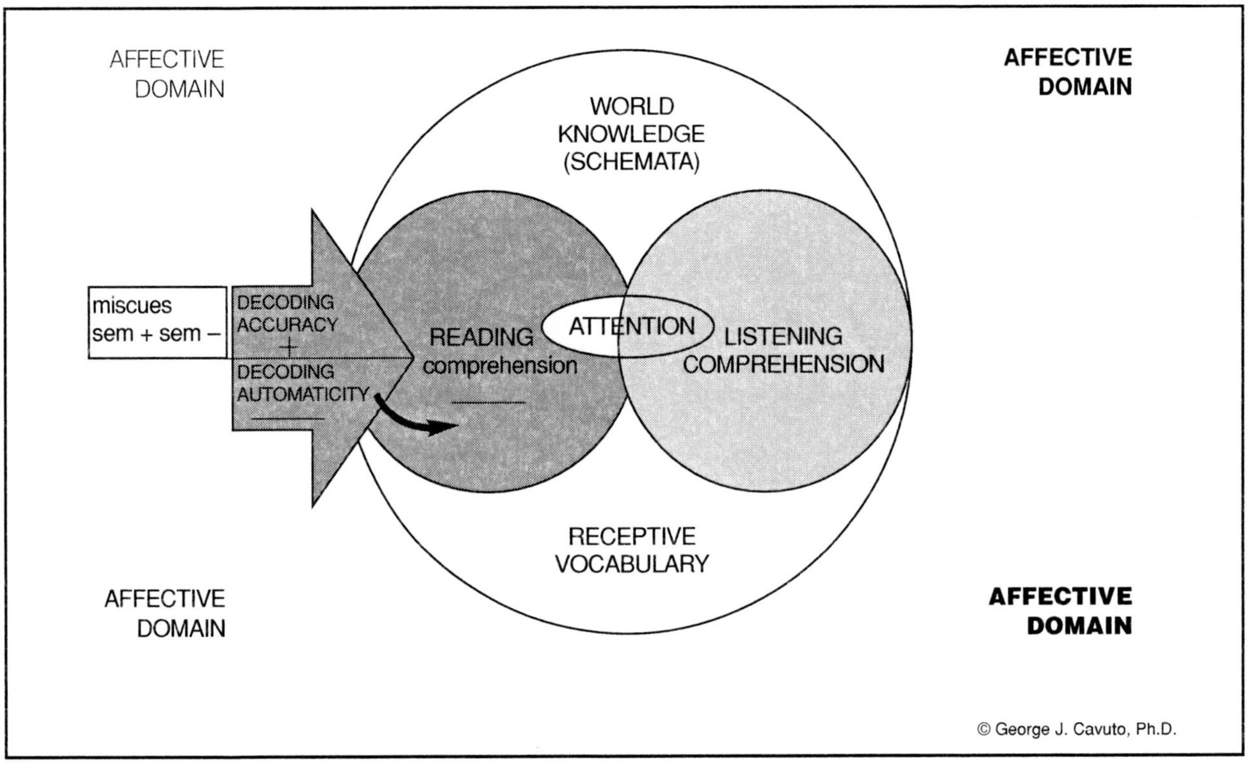

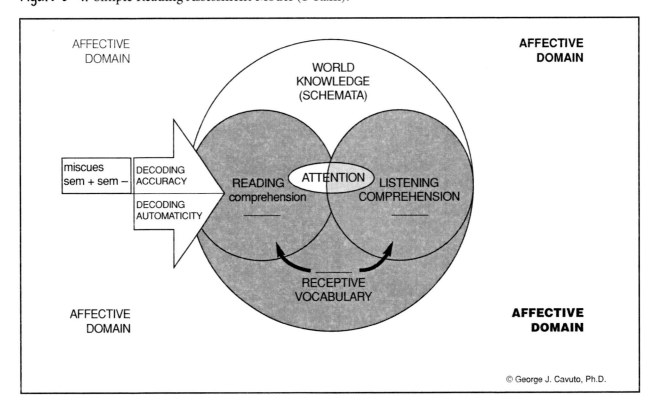

Figure 8-4. Simple Reading Assessment Model (S-Ram).

5. If a student has inadequate/poor world knowledge (-WK), one could reasonably predict that this student will have poor reading comprehension (-RC) and poor listening comprehension (-LC). When reading is viewed as an interactive process where the reader is simultaneously taking information from the text (bottom up processing) and bringing information to the text (top down processing), it only makes sense that a reader with a paucity of background knowledge will be forced to engage in much bottom-up processing as he/she attempts to process textual discourse; invariably, this kind of one-dimensional processing will result in poor reading comprehension. Similarly, the student who is listening to material (about which he/she has little background knowledge) being read to him/her, will have difficulty relating the incoming information to his/her existing cognitive structure (i.e., knowledge base); hence, his/her listening comprehension is also, most likely, going to be inadequate/poor. In formulaic form:

$$-WK \longrightarrow -RC \text{ and } -LC$$

In S-RAM form: (See Figure 8-5.)

Figure 8-5. Simple Reading Assessment Model (S-Ram).

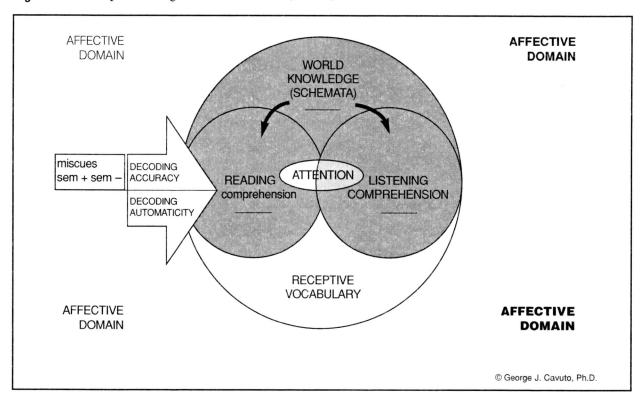

© George J. Cavuto, Ph.D.

6. If a student has inadequate/poor attention-concentration span (-A/C S), one could reasonably predict that this student will have poor reading comprehension (-RC) and poor listening comprehension (-LC). Both reading comprehension and listening comprehension require the student to hold incoming information in his/her short-term memory and then move it to long-term memory. A student who has a short-term memory deficit (i.e., difficulty sustaining attention/concentration) will most probably experience considerable difficulty remembering/understanding that which he/she has listened to or read; both of these processes require the ability to attend/concentrate. In formulaic form:

$$-A/C\ S \longrightarrow -RC\ and\ -LC$$

In S-RAM form: (See Figure 8-6.)

Figure 8-6. Simple Reading Assessment Model (S-Ram).

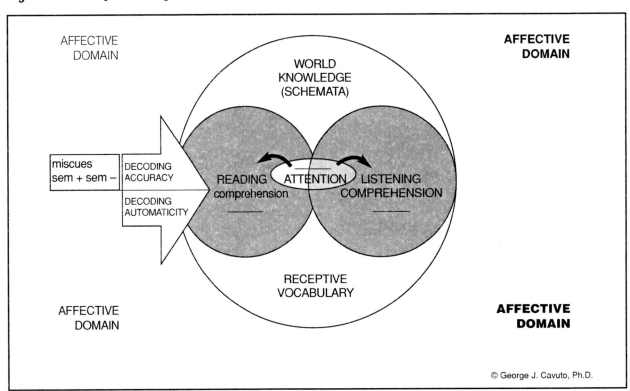

© George J. Cavuto, Ph.D.

7. If a student makes many miscues, particularly on key/concept words in a text, as he/she reads aloud, and these miscues tend to be high graphophonic, syntactically acceptable, and semantically unacceptable (SEM-) (and the student rarely, if ever, self-corrects these miscues), one could reasonably conclude that the student will have poor/inadequate reading comprehension (-RC). Semantically unacceptable miscues significantly distort the author's intended meaning (see chapter 3). If the student makes many semantically unacceptable miscues (SEM-) on key concept words in the passage, he/she is most likely not understanding that which he/she is reading. The student's failure to realize that these miscues significantly distort the meaning further indicates a lack of comprehension; this also indicates a lack of consistent self-monitoring (-SM). In formulaic form:

$$\text{SEM- and -SM} \longrightarrow \text{-RC}$$

In S-RAM form: (See Figure 8-7.)

Figure 8-7. Simple Reading Assessment Model (S-Ram).

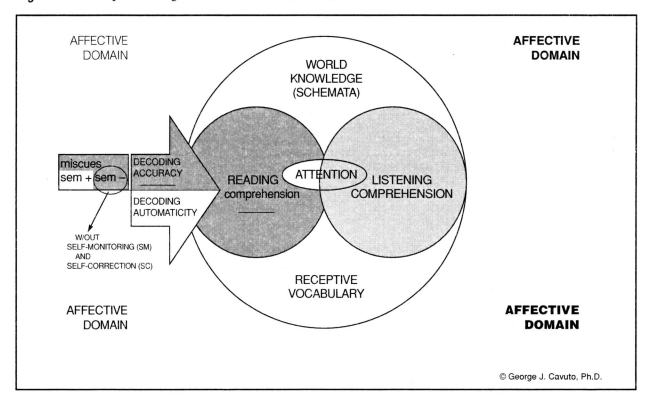

© George J. Cavuto, Ph.D.

8. If a student makes many miscues, particularly on key/concept words in a text, as he/she reads aloud, and these miscues tend to be high grapho-phonic, syntactically acceptable, and semantically unacceptable (SEM-), and the student consistently self-monitors (+SM) these miscues and then proceeds to self-correct (+SC) them, he/she is most likely understanding that which he/she has read. Clearly, in order to self-correct a meaning-changing miscue and replace it with a word that makes sense in the sentence/passage, the reader must be reading for meaning (i.e., processing the text at a deep structure level). In formulaic form:

SEM- and +SM and +SC $\longrightarrow$ +RC

In S-RAM form: (See Figure 8-8.)

Figure 8-8. Simple Reading Assessment Model (S-Ram).

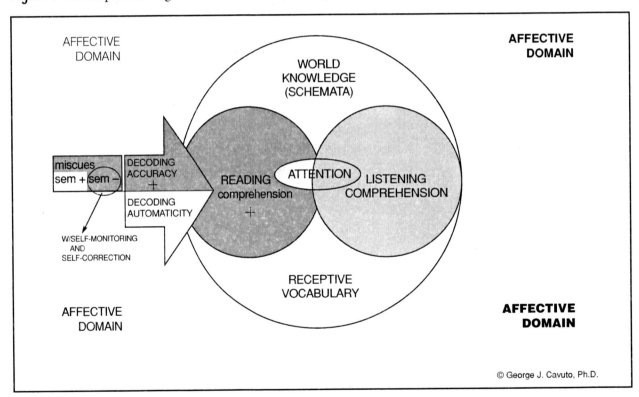

The inferences articulated above represent reasonable predictions about one aspect of the reading process based upon knowledge of a student's performance in other aspects of the process. Reading assessment is a problem solving activity; it involves a good degree of higher order thinking/reasoning skills. Inferential reasoning is a higher order cognitive process. I strongly believe that in order for teachers/specialists to become competent assessors of students' reading, they must begin to engage in this kind of problem solving cognitive process. This is not to suggest, however, that the aforementioned formuli (or S-RAMS) should be used in an unquestioning/unequivocal manner; rather, they should be used to make reasonable inferences/hypotheses about students' text processing which must then be either confirmed or disconfirmed based upon a significant amount of classroom-based observations of the students as they engage in authentic reading tasks.

FOLLOW-UP EXERCISES

1. When Max, a third-grade student, reads aloud he makes lots of miscues (on key words in the text) that significantly distort the author's intended meaning. These miscues are rarely, if ever, self-corrected. What reasonable inference can you make about Max's reading comprehension? Explain your answer.

2. Miguel, a seventh-grade student, has excellent receptive vocabulary. What reasonable inference, if any, can you make about Miguel's background knowledge (schemata)? Explain your answer. What reasonable inference, if any, can you make about Miguel's word identification/decoding accuracy? What reasonable inference, if any, can you make about Miguel's word identification/decoding automaticity? Explain your answers.

3. Heidi, a second-grade student, makes many semantically unacceptable miscues as she reads; she rarely, if ever, self-corrects these miscues. What inference, if any, could you make about Heidi's self-monitoring skills? Explain your answer. What inference, if any, could you make about Heidi's reading comprehension? What inference, if any, could you make about Heidi's listening comprehension? Explain your answers.

4. Cindy, a ninth grade student, decodes words accurately; however, she does not recognize the words in her content area textbooks immediately (i.e., she mediates extensively.) What reasonable inference, if any, could you make about Cindy's reading comprehension? What inference, if any, could you make about Cindy's listening comprehension? What inference, if any, could you make about Cindy's background knowledge? Explain your answers.

5. Bernard, a sixth-grade student, has significant gaps in his experiential background. What inference, if any, could you make about Bernard's reading comprehension? What inference, if any, could you make about Bernard's listening comprehension? What inference, if any, could you make about Bernard's receptive vocabulary? Explain your answers.

6. Joshua is in the third grade. His oral reading is fast and fluent; however, he tends to miscue on many key words when reading his content area textbooks; these miscues are usually semantically unacceptable. Joshua then proceeds to self-correct each of the miscues. What reasonable inference, if any, could you make about Joshua's reading comprehension? What reasonable inference, if any, could you make about Joshua's word identification/decoding accuracy? What reasonable inference, if any, could you make about Joshua's word identification/decoding automaticity? What reasonable inference, if any, could you make about Joshua's receptive vocabulary? Explain your answers.

7. Kim, a fourth-grade student, has very poor reading comprehension. What inference, if any, could you make about her receptive vocabulary? What inference, if any, could you make about her world knowledge/experiential background? What inference, if any, could you make about her word identification/decoding automaticity? Explain your answers.

8. Shawn is in the first grade. He has very poor word identification/decoding skills. What inference, if any, could you make about Shawn's word identification/decoding automaticity? What inference, if any, could you make about Shawn's reading comprehension? What inference, if any, could you make about Shawn's listening comprehension? What inference, if any, could you make about Shawn's receptive vocabulary? Explain your answers.

Ascertaining Functional Reading Levels

functional reading levels, independent reading level, instructional reading level,
frustration reading level, Betts' criteria

Although reading experts generally agree that reading levels are not, and indeed should not be considered exact indicators of a student's reading performance, they are, nonetheless, helpful for many reasons:

1. They help teachers better understand the degree to which students are able to read their content area textbooks

2. They help the teachers guide students to appropriate books for independent reading; and, (perhaps, most importantly)

3. They give all shareholders concerned with a student's academic performance (i.e., the student himself/herself, the student's parents/caretakers, classroom teachers, educational specialists) a realistic view of how the student will perform when attempting to process grade appropriate textual information.

Clearly, reading levels are oftentimes arrived at using mostly quantitative information; however, qualitative information should also be used in determining a student's functional reading levels. Betts was one of the first reading experts to articulate a criteria for the three *functional reading levels* (Betts, 1946). Over the years, Betts' criteria has been *modified* by literacy specialists; this has been done in the development of Informal Reading Inventories.

According to many Informal Reading Inventories, text is at a reader's *independent level* if he/she is able to correctly decode (i.e., word recognition/decoding accuracy) 95 percent or more of the text words (counting semantically acceptable miscues as correct*) and has at least 90 percent comprehension of the text; text is at a reader's *instructional level* if he/she can correctly decode at least 90 percent of the words in the text (counting semantically acceptable miscues as correct*) and has 70 percent or better comprehension of the text; and the text is at a *frustration level* if the reader's word identification/decoding accuracy is less than 90 percent (counting semantically acceptable miscues as correct*) or if his/her reading comprehension of the text is less than 70 percent.

Level	Word Identification/ Decoding Accuracy		Reading Comprehension
independent	95% or better	AND	90% or better
instructional	90% or better	AND	70% or better
frustration	less than 90%	OR	less than 70%

[*this was not part of Betts' original criteria; it has been added to the criteria by numerous reading experts based upon the work done by K. Goodman and Y. Goodman.]

A long held axiom of reading pedagogy is as follows: Whenever possible, try to teach the student with a text that is at his/her reading instructional level; try to encourage recreational reading with books that are at the student's *independent level*; and do the best that you can to avoid texts that are at the student's frustration level; however, if this cannot be done (and often it can't, especially considering the fact that content area textbooks are typically written one year above the grade in which they are used), then it is incumbent upon the teacher to utilize pre-, during, and post-content area reading strategies to help the student(s) more effectively cope with frustration level texts.

Clearly, effective reading assessment MUST involve a combination of both quantitative and qualitative information. Our present, legitimate concern with, and emphasis on, qualitative information in reading has led us to do one of two things with quantitative information:

1. totally ignore a discussion of a student's functional reading levels and limit the assessment information to qualitative information only;

2. replace the functional reading levels (independent, instructional, frustration levels) with somewhat ambiguous, qualitative terms (e.g., early emergent, advanced emergent, early beginning, advanced beginning, early independent, advanced independent). (The University of the State of New York, 1997.)

Unfortunately, my experience and discussions with teachers suggests that this hasn't achieved the desired objective of encouraging teachers to concentrate less on quantitatively assessing their students' reading performance and focusing more on qualitative aspects; instead, teachers have been expending much time and energy attempting to disambiguate the aforementioned new qualitative terms. Rather than focusing on aspects of a student's reading processing, too many teachers are trying to decide, for example, whether Johnny/Jill is at the "early emergent," "advanced emergent," "early beginning," "advanced beginning," (NYSED Early Literacy Profile Document) stage of reading. In many cases, this kind of decision MUST be made because it satisfies state standards; it must also be made because these terms appear on the child's report card. Interestingly enough, these stages mean very little to parents and hence provide them with, at best, limited information and, at worst, misleading information re: their child's reading ability.

By ascertaining a student's approximate functional reading levels, a teacher is well postured to make further assessment and instructional decisions regarding this student. For example, if a third-grade student is functioning at a 2-1 (i.e., first half of second grade) instructional level, there should be no mystery as to why this student is experiencing considerable difficulty reading his science, social studies, and literature anthology texts. These texts are probably written close to a 4th-grade level; the student's reading instructional level is approximately 2-1; this represents approximately a two year gap! This is very important information of which all shareholders in the child's academic life should be cognizant. Without this information, it is simply too easy to draw conclusions that may, in fact, be incorrect (e.g., the child is simply "lazy," or "immature," perhaps he/she has a "learning disability," maybe he/she is simply "a late bloomer"). I have heard each of the aforementioned used to (incorrectly) describe children's reading performance. It has been my experience that when there is more than a year's disparity between a student's reading instructional level and his/her grade placement, invariably the student encounters rather significant difficulty succeeding with his/her schoolwork. This is important to know. Clearly, knowing about qualitative aspects of this student's reading/language processing (e.g., by using the S-RAM) is going to be more important in terms of developing an instructional program for the student; however, having some idea as to the student's approximate functional reading levels is information that will also inform the instructional plan and hence should be given consideration as well.

Several researchers and organizations (Guidry and Knight, 1976; College Entrance Examination Board, 1982; Fountas and Pinnell, 1999) have evaluated the approximate readability of literally thousands of fiction and nonfiction texts. By consulting these important resources, teachers can help students make viable choices of books that they would like to read and, indeed, can read!

Reading assessment is by no means an exact science and I am not suggesting that it is; however, it is also not a science without generally accepted assessment and instructional guidelines (e.g., Betts' criteria). Criteria do exist and thus it only makes sense that all teachers and administrators are aware of these guidelines as one source of assessment information.

ASCERTAINING A STUDENT'S READING INSTRUCTIONAL LEVEL

If a student is able to read, for example, a text that has a fifth-grade readability level with 90 percent or better word recognition/decoding accuracy and 70 percent or better reading comprehension, then we would say that this student's reading instructional level is fifth grade; or stated differently, this text is at the student's reading instructional level.

When using the aforementioned Informal Reading Inventory (IRI) criteria to ascertain a student's functional reading levels, it is quite possible for the teacher to find that a student has more than one instructional level (perhaps even several). For example, let's assume that a teacher's everyday observations of Sandy's reading indicates that she can correctly identify/decode (counting semantically acceptable miscues as correct) 3-1 material with 95 percent accuracy and her comprehension at this level is consistently between 70–80 percent (using the chart on page 130, this would indicate instructional level); however, the teacher has also observed that Sandy's performance is approximately the same (i.e., 90 percent word identification/decoding accuracy and 70–75 percent comprehension) when reading 3-2 level texts. When this happens, a general rule of thumb is to consider the highest instructional level (in this case, 3-2) to be the actual instructional reading level . If, for example, a student has instructional levels of 4, 5, and 6, 6 should be considered his/her actual instructional reading level. Like all instructional decisions, the decision to consider a student's highest reading instructional level to be the level at which he/she will receive instruction is theoretically/philosophically based; it reflects the belief that students should be given materials that challenge them. Why choose a 4th grade instructional level for a student when he/she can handle a 6th grade text with approximately the same degree of success?

ASCERTAINING A STUDENT'S INDEPENDENT READING LEVEL

If a student is able to read, for example, a text that has a second-grade readability level with 95 percent or better word recognition/decoding accuracy and 90 percent or better reading comprehension, then we would say that this student's independent reading level is second grade; or stated differently, this text is at the student's independent reading level.

If a student appears to have more than one independent reading level (using Betts' criteria), a general rule of thumb would be to choose the highest one of these levels and consider this level the student's independent reading level; however, if this student also had several instructional reading levels, and you chose the highest one of these as his/her actual instructional reading level (as was recommended above), then the next highest level would/could be considered the student's independent reading level (even though the student's performance at this level didn't satisfy Betts' criteria for this level). This is why I continually make the point that reading assessment is not an exact science!

ASCERTAINING A STUDENT'S FRUSTRATION READING LEVEL

If a student reads, for example, a text that has an eighth-grade readability level with less than 70 percent reading comprehension (regardless of his/her word recognition/decoding accuracy), then we would say that this text is at the student's frustration level. If the previous level of difficulty (i.e., seventh-grade) had been ascertained as being this student's reading instructional level, then eighth-grade would be considered the student's frustration level. If a student reads the same level text (eighth-grade) with 80 percent comprehension but only 80 percent word recognition/decoding accuracy (counting semantically acceptable miscues as correct), then this book would be considered at a frustration level for this student (using a strict application of IRI criteria); however, when this happens (i.e., the student meets the comprehension part of the criteria but fails to meet the word recognition/decoding accuracy part of the criteria), the teacher may decide, upon further, ongoing qualitative analysis of the student's performance, to give less emphasis to the word recognition/decoding accuracy parameter in Betts' criteria and give primary consideration to the reading comprehension variable. Once again, this decision would be clearly reflective of the teacher's philosophy of reading (i.e., that comprehension/meaning is always the most important part of the literacy assessment/instruction equation).

If a fourth-grade student, for example, is functioning at a frustration level when reading third-grade level text, we would consider third grade to be his/her frustration level. Clearly, his/her instructional reading level and independent reading level would be BELOW this level; therefore, to say that he has frustration levels at third- and fourth-grade levels would be unnecessary/redundant. When we state that a student's frustration level is third-grade level, there would be a clear implication that all levels above this would be equally, if not more frustrating. Hence, the first frustration level reached after the highest instructional level is usually referred to as the student's actual frustration level.

SUMMARY

Ascertaining a student's functional reading levels is ONE important part of an overall assessment of his/her reading. It is an important part of the assessment and should not be overlooked; however, we should be reminded that the most valid reading assessments are:

1. conducted over time

2. based on the student's actual reading of authentic textual information

3. informed by both qualitative and quantitative information (including standardized test information and the student's functional reading levels)

4. done by a professional who has an in-depth theoretical and pragmatic understanding of reading/language processes (i.e., one with the "knowing eye and knowing ear") [Cavuto, 1992].

Even with each of these factors in place, a reading assessment should always be considered tentative because exemplary reading assessment is ongoing; all reading assessments should be seen as tentative hypotheses to be confirmed, disconfirmed, or confirmed with modifications as more information, both qualitative and quantitative, is gathered. Clearly, reading assessment is a dynamic, problem solving process.

FOLLOW-UP EXERCISES

1. Henry, an eighth-grade student, reads his eighth-grade science text with approximately 98 percent word identification/decoding accuracy (counting semantically acceptable miscues as correct); his reading comprehension of this text is consistently in the 90–100 percent range. Is this text at Henry's independent reading level, instructional reading level, or frustration level? Based upon the aforementioned information, how would you expect Henry to do if he were asked to read a chapter of this text at home and answer the "End of Chapter Questions" without receiving any help? Explain your answers.

2. Paige is in the fourth grade. Her teacher has observed the following: When Paige reads her social studies and science textbooks, her word identification/decoding accuracy (counting semantically acceptable miscues as correct) is approximately 90 percent; her reading comprehension of these texts is consistently in the 50–60 percent range. Is this text at Paige's independent reading level, instructional reading level, or frustration level? Based upon the aforementioned information, how would Paige do if asked to read a chapter of this text at home (without receiving any help) and answer the "End of the Chapter Questions"? Explain your answers.

3. William, a third-grade student, makes a significant number of semantically unacceptable miscues (more than 30 percent) when reading his literature anthology; he does not self-correct these miscues. His reading comprehension of this text is consistently in the 50–60 percent range. Would you say that this book is at William's independent, instructional, or frustration level? Explain your answer.

4. Elizabeth's fifth-grade teacher has made the following observation about her reading: "When reading her science and social studies texts, Elizabeth miscues rarely, if ever; her reading comprehension is consistently in the 85–90 percent range." Based upon this very limited observation, what would you predict is Elizabeth's approximate reading instructional level? Explain your answer.

5. Jason is a seventh-grade student. His teacher has been experimenting with several different "trade books" in an attempt to ascertain Jason's approximate functional reading levels. When she gives him books at approximately a fifth-grade readability level, she finds that his word identification/decoding accuracy (counting semantically acceptable miscues as correct) is approximately 90–95 percent; his reading comprehension at this level is consistently 75–80 percent. When his teacher gives Jason books at approximately the 6th grade level, his word identification/decoding accuracy (counting semantically acceptable miscues as correct) is approximately 90 percent; his reading comprehension at this level is consistently in the 70 percent range. When Jason is given trade books that are written at approximately the seventh grade level, his word identification/decoding accuracy (counting semantically acceptable miscues as correct) is approximately 90 percent; his reading comprehension at this level is almost always less than 60 percent. Based upon this information, what would you say is Jason's independent reading level? What would you say is Jason's instructional reading level? What would you say is Jason's frustration level? If you were conducting a Reader's Workshop in your class (i.e., where you taught your students specific reading strategies through the literature that they were reading), what level trade book would be appropriate for Jason to read for this part of your classroom instruction? What level trade book would you send home for Jason to read on his own? Explain your answers.

References

Betts, E.A. (1946). *Foundations of Reading Instruction.* New York: American Book Company.

Cavuto, George. (1992, October/November). "Kidwatching: Helping Teachers Develop the Knowing Eye." *Reading Today,* p. 28.

College Entrance Examination Board. *Degrees of Reading Power* (Readability Report, 1982–83 academic year). New York: The College Board, 1982.

Fountas, I.C. & Pinnell, G.S. (1999). Matching books to readers: Using leveled books in guided reading K–3. Portsmouth, NH: Heinemann.

Guidry. L.J. & Knight, D.F. (1976). "Comparative readability: Four Formulas and Newbery Books." *Journal of Reading,* 19, 552–556.

———. (1997). *English Language Arts Resource Guide.* The University of the State of New York, The State Education Department.

CHAPTER 10

Sharing Reading Assessments

Key Words/Terms

education shareholders, ownership of literacy, external locus of control, passive failure in reading, vocalizations

As has been stated previously in this text, the primary purpose of reading assessment is to inform instruction; if the assessment doesn't inform instruction it is of little use or value to any of the education shareholders (e.g., student, parents/caretakers, teachers, administrators). Once a reading assessment has been made, (hopefully, over time based upon much naturalistic assessment and, perhaps, informed by more formal assessments as well), this assessment should be shared with:

1. the student (Note: it is critically important for the student to be made aware of his/her strengths/weaknesses in reading so that he/she can become a "willing partner" in the plan to capitalize on his/her strengths in order to remediate weaknesses);

2. the student's parents/caretakers;

3. other education shareholders/professionals involved in the student's instructional program (e.g., literacy specialists, special educators, school administrators, school/private psychologists, speech/language pathologists).

SHARING RESULTS OF A READING ASSESSMENT WITH THE STUDENT

For many years, there was a mentality in some education circles that teachers assess students' reading and then keep this assessment to themselves! Indeed, oftentimes when a particularly inquisitive student queried, "How did I do on that?" the response would be, "Fine, fine" regardless of the student's actual performance. In the past two decades, there has been much research dealing with students' "ownership of their own literacy" (Harp, 1999). Clearly, if the student is to have "ownership" of his/her literacy, it is very important that he/she be made aware of both strengths and weaknesses.

It is a basic premise of learning theory that in order to improve at any activity, human beings need adequate and appropriate feedback. It is the teacher's responsibility to provide each of his/her students with specific information regarding that student's performance in each and every aspect of the reading/language process. This feedback is important for all students; however, it is critically important for students who are experiencing reading difficulties.

A second-grade student, for example, who has significant difficulty in word identification/decoding accuracy, may believe that he/she is "stupid" because of this inadequacy; indeed, this youngster may, in fact, be quite intelligent (i.e., excellent world knowledge/schemata); this student is embarrassed when he/she is called upon to read aloud in class: he/she struggles to figure out the words and the other children sometimes laugh and the teacher seems to become somewhat annoyed. He/she has also learned that when he/she sits down to read to his/her parents at home, they also seem to become somewhat "upset" by his/her inability to read the words correctly; they tell him, "Sound it out"; he tries, but often to no avail.

Is there any reason whatsoever why this student shouldn't believe that he/she isn't stupid? The statement, "knowledge is power" seems to be particularly appropriate here: If the student possesses the knowledge of what it is that he/she cannot do, and indeed can do, as he/she attempts to process printed information, then he/she will have the power to "partner" with his/her teachers and parents/caretakers to "fix" the problem(s). Conversely, without this kind of understanding, he/she is left to concoct reasons to explain his/her poor reading: (e.g., "I forgot my glasses"; "This book is boring"; "I didn't learn anything last year with Mrs. Brown, she was out a lot"; "I'm stupid!") This student has developed what has been called an "external locus of control" (Williams, M. and Williams, H., 1992). He/she blames "externals" for his/her reading failure. Johnston and Winograd (1985) suggest that this student is experiencing "passive failure" in reading. Clearly, until the student takes responsibility for his/her own reading weaknesses, there is little, if any chance, of overcoming them. Hence, the first step in helping a student to improve his/her reading/language skills/strategies is to make an informed assessment of the student's strengths and weaknesses and then share this information with the student in an honest and candid manner.

Instead of free-floating, amorphic, mysterious demons, reading difficulties should be *disambiguated*. The teacher should be able to sit down with each student in his/her class and, with the Simple Reading Assessment Model (S-RAM) clearly visible to both of them, explain to the student, in language appropriate to the age/grade of the student, those aspects of the reading/language process at which the student performs well (+'s) and those aspects that need improvement (–'s). If reading comprehension is a problem, the teacher should be able to provide the student with specific "causation(s)" (explicit and/or implicit) for his/her reading comprehension difficulties. The teacher should then explain to the student the kinds of things that he/she will be doing in class with the student (i.e., his/her instructional plan) to help remediate the weaknesses; he/she should also talk to the student about the kinds of things that he/she will have to do at home in order to improve. It is very important that the student perceives himself/herself as an active participant in the process; this is both enlightening and empowering for the student.

I have found that students are far more willing to become active "partners" in their reading instructional program IF the aforementioned "assessment sharing" is done with them. I've worked with several children, for example, who had very poor word identification/decoding accuracy, very poor word identification decoding automaticity, very poor reading comprehension, excellent receptive vocabulary, excellent world knowledge, and excellent listening comprehension. (See Figure 10-1.)

These students literally "lit up" when I explained both their strengths and weaknesses to them; they were very pleased when I let them know that their ability to understand material read to them was a grade or two above their actual

Figure 10-1. Simple Reading Assessment Model (S-Ram).

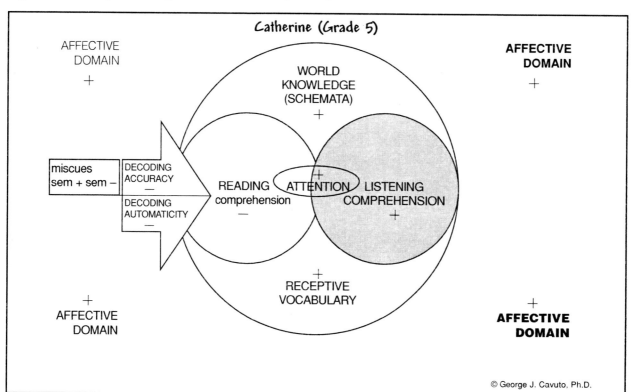

grade placements; several had that look in their eyes that said, "So I'm not so dumb after all!" When I clearly explained that their major problem was figuring out the words and that this difficulty was making it difficult/impossible for them to understand that which they had read, this simple, rational explanation seemed to make sense to them; it was almost as if they already understood this, even the youngest students, on an unconscious level. I had simply confirmed that which had already crossed their minds; however, my confirmation was critically important—it had greater importance; I'm the teacher!

You may be asking, at this point, "What about those students who have minuses (–'s) in EVERY section of the Simple Reading Assessment Model? What do you tell them?" Obviously, there are a significant number of students who have difficulty in every aspect of the reading/language process. I am a firm believer in "academic/intellectual honesty"; we shouldn't lie to these students and tell them that they are doing "fine" when every aspect of their daily performance in school belies this statement; to do so would be disingenuous. Students must have a very clear sense that their teacher is going to tell them the truth, good or bad! For this reason, I believe that even students with multiple deficits should have each area explained to them; the teacher's classroom-based and home-based instructional plan should be shared with them; and their roles/responsibilities should be shared with them as well. Perhaps the child with multiple deficits in the reading/language process is motivated, enthusiastic, and persevering. If this were actually the case, I would place a huge plus (+) in the Affective Domain part of the Simple Reading Assessment Model; I would let the student know that this is a very important strength that will help him/her to improve in all of the other areas.

SHARING THE RESULTS OF A READING ASSESSMENT WITH PARENTS/CARETAKERS

Just as students are entitled to a rational, informed, quantitative and qualitative assessment of their reading/language skills strategies, similarly, parents/caretakers have an equal right to this information. In my experience, all too often, parents/caretakers are given vague, incomplete, misleading, and sometimes even incorrect information about their child's reading/language skills/strategies. We must do better! I suggest that teachers have a Simple Reading Assessment Model (S-RAM) in front of them (with +'s and –'s clearly visible) when discussing a student's reading with his/her parents/caretakers. I further suggest that the teacher begin the discussion by showing the parents/caretakers the Simple Reading Assessment Model (S-RAM) and letting them know that he/she has been assessing their youngster's reading (using both formal and informal/observational assessments) over the past several months, and would like to take this opportunity to share with them their youngster's reading/language Strengths and Weaknesses.

Having said this, I strongly recommend that the teacher start this sharing of information by explaining those reading/language (or affective domain) areas that are Strengths for the particular student in question. The teacher must remember that regardless of the parents'/caretakers' level of education, some of the terms we teachers use will be somewhat new to them; this doesn't mean that they shouldn't be used; however, it does mean that it is incumbent upon us to explain these terms in clear, simple, unambiguous language:

(Example: "Mr. and Mrs. Smith, I'd like to start by talking to you about one of your son Peter's strengths in the reading/language process: He has a definite strength in the area of word identification/decoding accuracy. Word identification and decoding mean the same thing—the terms are used interchangeably. They both refer to a reader's ability to look at a written word and somehow "break the code"/ say the word. If Peter were to look at the written word "basketball" and read it as "basketball," we would say that he had accurate word identification/decoding. Conversely, if he were to look at the written word "basketball," and read it as "batball," we would say that he had decoded/identified this word incorrectly. Word identification/decoding accuracy, in very simple terms, has to do with Peter's ability to translate written information into spoken information. If he is reading aloud, the listener would hear the written words being said; if he is reading silently, the written words are being translated into oral language that he is simply not verbalizing (note: sometimes readers engage in what we call *vocalizations* during silent reading; this occurs when the child is reading silently; however, the listener can actually hear the words being verbalized.) It is important to remember, Mr. and Mrs. Smith, that word identification/decoding accuracy simply has to do with whether or not Peter is able to "figure out the words—break the code"; it is different from knowing what those words mean. Knowing, or not knowing, their meaning has to do with another area that we'll be talking about in a little while; this area of the reading process is called *receptive vocabulary*. Okay, so before we move on I want to be very sure that you understand that in this aspect of the reading/language process that we call word identification/decoding accuracy, your son Peter is doing very nicely. He is able to accurately decode/identify most of the words found in grade-level texts; indeed, my classroom assessment of Peter's decoding/word identification accuracy appears to indicate that Peter is functioning approximately two years above his grade-level placement in this aspect of the reading process. As we all know, Peter is in the fifth grade; I have found that his decoding/word identification accuracy is approximately seventh-grade level; clearly, this is a strength for Peter. Indeed, we like to see a youngster's decoding/word identification accuracy at least one year above his/her grade level placement since content area textbooks (e.g., science, social studies textbooks) are typically written one full reading level above the grade in which they are being used. We refer to this as the *one-year cushion in decoding/word identification accuracy*. Peter most certainly has this cushion; indeed, he has a two-year cushion. Before we move on to the next aspect of Peter's reading/language processing, do you have any questions about Peter's decoding/word identification accuracy?"

Although explanations of each aspect of the reading process (i.e., each section of the Simple Reading Assessment Model [S-RAM]) may take some time , it is critically important to do this. Parents/caretakers MUST be made aware of their child's strengths and weaknesses in reading in as detailed and straightforward a manner as possible; this is impossible to do without carefully explaining each aspect of the reading process. I have found that parents/caretakers are very pleased when this kind of detailed explanation is given to them; indeed, it has been my experience that even parents/caretakers of children who have many weaknesses (–'s) in reading are thankful that someone is taking the time to explain exactly why Johnny/Jill is having such difficulty in reading. Oftentimes, the explanations that I have given to parents of children who are experiencing considerable difficulty learning to read simply confirm their own beliefs based upon their experience observing the youngster attempting to process printed text: "You're right on target! Johnny gets very upset when he has to read out loud to me for fifteen minutes a night; he hates it; however, he loves when my wife or I read to him. I guess this is because, as you said, he has inadequate word identification/decoding accuracy but excellent listening comprehension; that makes a lot of sense and is perfectly consistent with that which we are seeing at home every night."

Conversely, there have been occasions when explaining a child's reading strengths and weaknesses to the parents/caretakers, that I get the feeling that they were really quite confused as to what was going on with the child re: the reading process. In these cases I'm very careful to relate my formal and informal assessments of their child's reading to their own observations at home: "Juanita has very poor word identification/decoding accuracy—she has lots of difficulty figuring out the words as she reads. Do you see this at home when she reads to you?" This kind of validation does two things

1. it helps increase the credibility of your assessment of the student's reading strengths and weaknesses;

2. it clearly makes the point that the student's reading experiences at home with the parents/caretakers is important . . . literacy is not simply a school phenomenon, it is a cultural phenomenon! (Heath, 1991)

SHARING THE RESULTS OF A READING ASSESSMENT WITH OTHER EDUCATION SHAREHOLDERS

Once each section of the Simple Reading Assessment Model (S-RAM) has been identified as either a strength (+) or a weakness (–) for the student, and, if reading comprehension is a weakness, the explicit and/or inferred causation has been established (based on much informal/classroom based assessment and perhaps some formal assessment(s) as well), the teacher is then in a position to logically and unambiguously share his/her assessment with other education shareholders (e.g., literacy specialist, special educator, speech/language pathologist). There may be some occasions where a teacher is unsure, based upon his/her classroom-based observations, as to whether a certain aspect of reading/language is a strength or weakness for the student. In such cases, he/she may consult a specialist in the area (e.g., the speech/language pathologist would be particularly well-trained to assess the student's receptive vocabulary) to help with this assessment. If, perhaps, the student is being considered for special education services , the classroom teacher (with the completed Simple Reading Assessment Model) is well-prepared to discuss the student's strengths and weaknesses in word identification/decoding accuracy, word identification/decoding automaticity, receptive vocabulary, world knowledge (schemata), listening comprehension, attention/concentration span, the affective domain, as well as causation for possible reading and/or listening comprehension weaknesses. This detailed information in every aspect of the reading/language process will be invaluable in helping the District Committee on Special Education to make appropriate placement decisions. Indeed, if the specialists were to complete and compare Simple Reading Assessment Models (S-RAMS) based upon their informal and formal assessments of the youngster's reading/language skills/strategies, comparisons could then be made between and among the different educators' assessments (i.e., +'s and −'s in each of the different sections of their Simple Reading Assessment Models). This could be extremely helpful in terms of deciding upon an appropriate intervention strategy for a student experiencing academic difficulty. All too often, such intervention has as its primary assessment, formal, norm-referenced, standardized, "one moment in time" assessments. Although these tests/instruments are not without merit, they are clearly not as valid as "ongoing" assessment over time. Many literacy specialists (Valencia, Hiebert, and Afferblach, 1994) agree that a combination of informal and formal assessments provide the "best of both worlds."

FOLLOW-UP EXERCISES

Examine each of the Simple Reading Assessment Models (S-RAMS) that follow. (See Figures 10-2–10-6.) Based upon the strengths (+'s) and weaknesses (–'s) indicated on each, practice discussing/verbalizing the following for each of three possible audiences:

1. the student;

2. the student's parents/caretakers;

3. other educational shareholders (e.g., school literacy specialist, special education teacher, administrators).
   a.) the student's reading/language strengths
   b.) the student's reading/language weaknesses
   c.) if reading comprehension and/or listening comprehension is a weakness, discuss both primary and secondary (if applicable) causations for the weakness; also, discuss whether the causation is explicit or inferred.

Figure 10-2. Simple Reading Assessment Model (S-Ram).

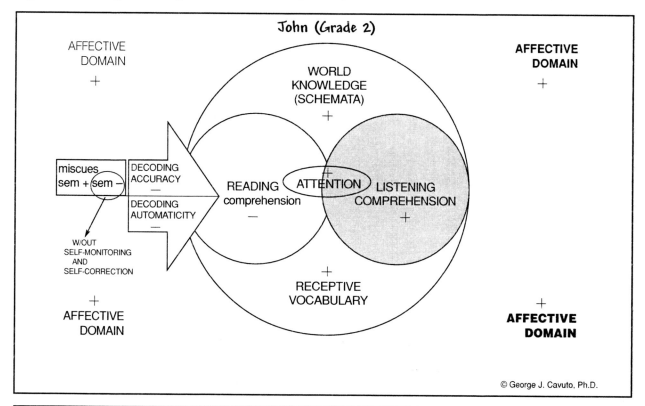

Figure 10-3. Simple Reading Assessment Model (S-Ram).

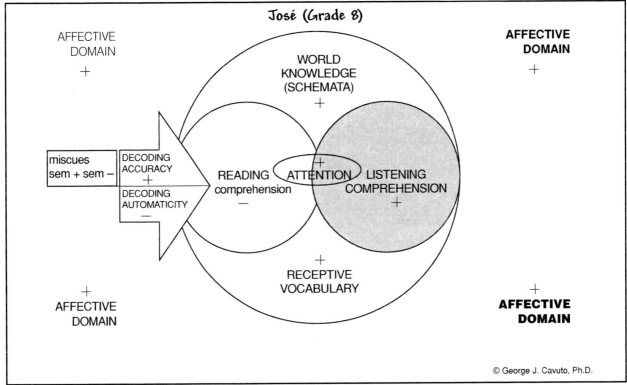

Figure 10-4. Simple Reading Assessment Model (S-Ram).

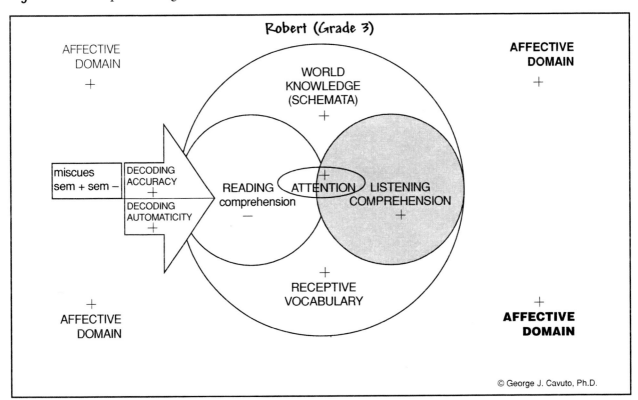

Figure 10-5. Simple Reading Assessment Model (S-Ram).

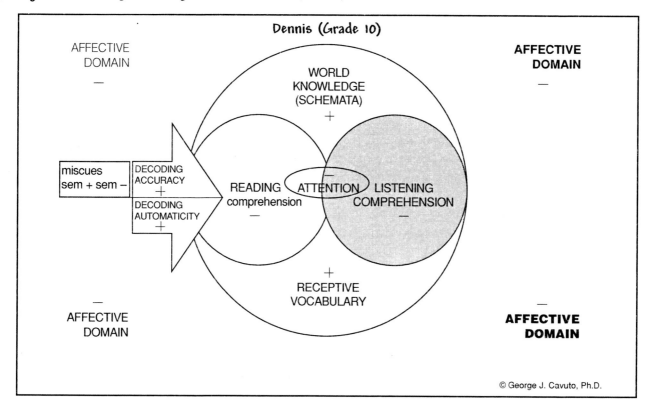

References

Harp, Bill (1991). "The whole language movement" (pp 1–16). In *Assessment and Evaluation in Whole Language Programs,* Bill Harp (Ed.). Norwood, MA: Christopher Gordon.

Heath, Shirley Brice (1991). "The sense of being literate" (pp. 3–25). In Rebecca Barr, Michael L. Kamil, Peter Mosenthal and P. David Pearson (Eds.). *Handbook of Reading Research Volume II.* New York: Longman.

Johnston, P. & Winograd, P. (1985). "Passive failure in reading." *Journal of Reading Behavior,* 17, 279–301.

Valencia, Sheila W., Hiebert, Elfrieda H., & Afflerbach, Peter P. (Eds.). (1994). Authentic Reading Assessment: Practices and Possibilities. Newark, DE: International Reading Association.

Williams, M., & Williams, H. "The relationship of locus of control and learned helplessness in special education students." *B.C. Journal of Special Education,* 16, 1–12.

CHAPTER 11

Reading Assessment Cases— Theory into Practice

Directions: After carefully reading and analyzing the information for each of the assessment cases, do the following:

1. Complete a Simple Reading Assessment Model (S-RAM) Chart (+'s and −'s as well as "causal arrows") for each case.

2. List and be prepared to discuss the student's literacy strengths.

3. List and be prepared to discuss the student's literacy weaknesses.

4. Discuss causation(s) for reading and/or listening comprehension inadequacies:

   • primary causation(s)? (explicit or inferred)?

   • secondary causation(s)? (explicit or inferred)?

5. Discuss the student's ability to use the language cueing systems (i.e., graphophonic, semantic, syntactic).

6. Discuss evidence of self-monitoring behaviors or lack thereof.

7. Identify any "disparate" (i.e., inconsistent, contradictory) information presented in the case narrative. If there is disparate information presented, are you able to logically "reconcile" this apparent disparity? If "yes," how? If "no," why not?

8. Make a decision as to whether or not further informal or formal assessment is needed before you are able to make even a "preliminary" assessment. Explain your answer.

CASE 1

Joseph is in the third grade. His teacher has made the following classroom-based observations of Joseph:

Joseph has significant difficulty reading the words in his content area textbooks; he frequently miscues and his miscues are almost always high graphophonic, syntactically acceptable, and semantically unacceptable. Joseph rarely, if ever, corrects these miscues; even the words that Joseph can read are decoded in a slow, methodical manner. Joseph has very poor comprehension following his reading of content area textbooks and grade-level literature chapter books; however, Joseph does enjoy our daily sessions when I read a book aloud to the class. During these sessions, Joseph is an active participant, often enthusiastically raising his hand to give the meaning of a vocabulary word or to answer a comprehension question—invariably, his answers are not only correct, but often show an incredible degree of insight into the text content; indeed, Joseph "shines" during these Read-Aloud Sessions. It usually takes Joseph an inordinate amount of time to finish his seatwork in all content areas except mathematics (Joseph is an excellent math student; he experiences math difficulties only in the area of word problems); he is able to stay on task for quite some time when doing math calculations; he is often the first to finish and usually has most of the calculation problems answered correctly. Unfortunately, when doing "seatwork" in science, social studies, and/or language arts, Joseph often squirms in his seat, drops his pencil, looks out the window, or attempts to engage another student in conversation; it appears that he has difficulty sustaining attention/concentration in these areas. Joseph is doing C–D work in all subjects except mathematics; he will earn a grade of B+ for this quarter's work in math. Joseph is not enthusiastic about choosing books to read from either our classroom library or the school library; he has to be encouraged to make a choice; I've heard him say, "I don't like to read books." Joseph's parents have indicated (during our first parent-teacher conference) that it is very difficult to get him to read at home; he would much rather they read to him!; they are getting frustrated trying to help him with his reading.

A group administered, standardized reading test was administered to Joseph (and his classmates) in May of second grade (approximately five months ago). Joseph scored as follows on this group administered, standardized testing instrument:

Word Identification:	*1.8 (grade level equivalent score);* *12th percentile*
Vocabulary:	*2.1 (grade level equivalent score)* *15th percentile*
Reading Comprehension:	*1.5 (grade level equivalent score)* *8th percentile*

Figure 11-1. Simple Reading Assessment Model (S-Ram).

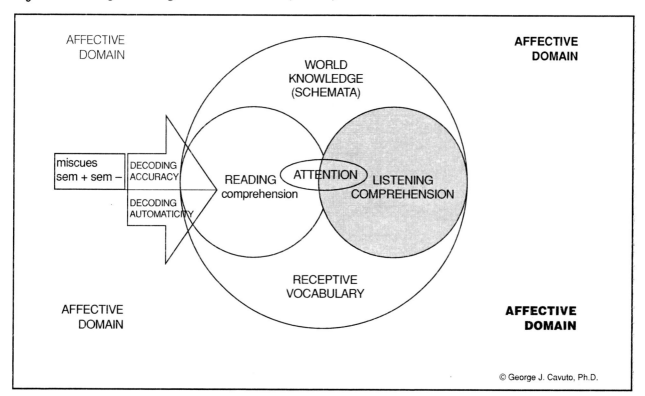

Reading Strengths:

Reading Weaknesses:

Primary Causations for Reading Comprehension Difficulty (if present): [w/explanation]

Secondary Causations for Reading Comprehension Difficulty (if present): [w/explanation]

Primary Causations for Listening Comprehension Difficulty (if present): [w/explanation]

Secondary Causations for Listening Comprehension Difficulty (if present): [w/explanation]

CASE 2

Kathleen is in the eighth grade. She is having difficulty in all of her subject areas. It takes her an enormous amount of time to do her homework assignments. Her English/language arts teacher has made the following observations:

Kathleen appears to have significant difficulty understanding concepts from the literature that we are reading; she reads fluently (and rarely makes errors) when called upon to do so in class; however, she does not contribute to discussions about the literary work and has significant difficulty answering my questions (both literal and interpretive) when called upon to do so. Kathleen appears to be trying, but to no avail. Her contributions to discussions about the novel that I read to the class every day are also minimal; she also has difficulty answering specific questions about the novel being read to the class. She appears to have a limited knowledge of words and the concepts represented by these words. She does appear to have the ability to stay on task. Her facial expressions appear to clearly indicate that she is experiencing considerable frustration.

Figure 11-2. Simple Reading Assessment Model (S-Ram).

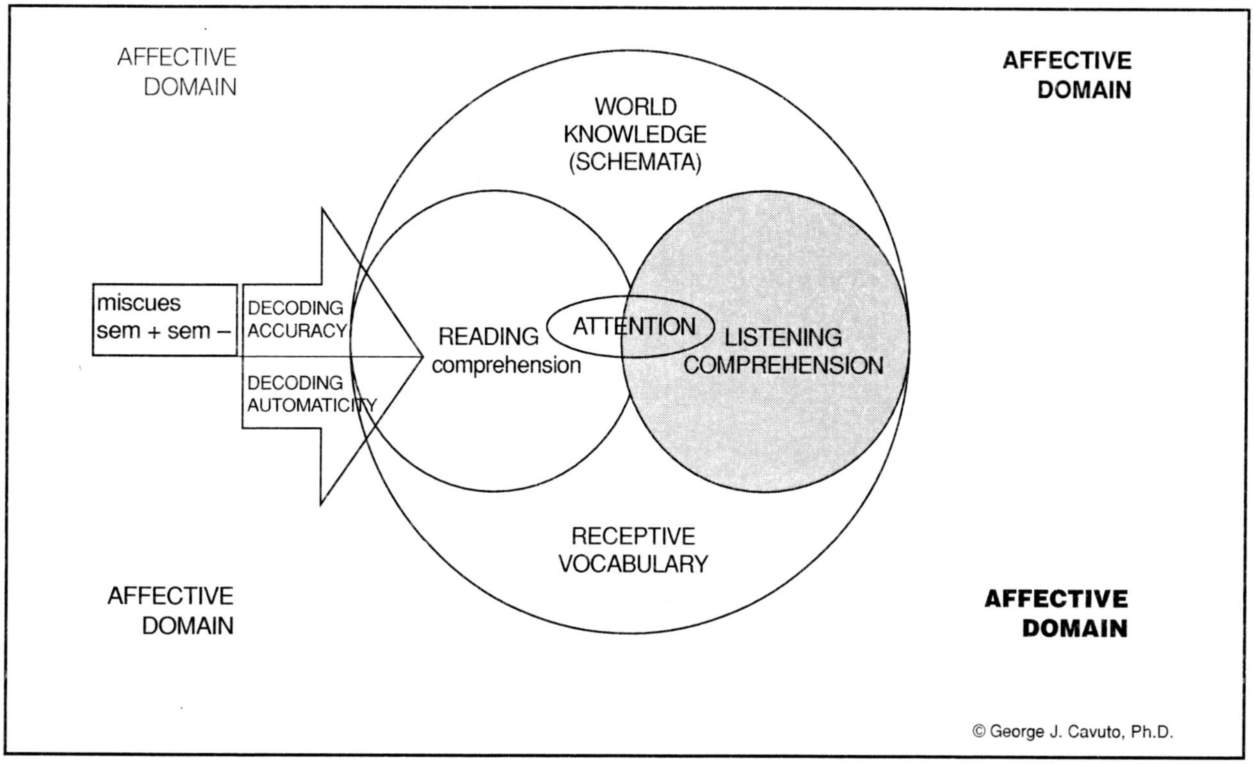

AFFECTIVE DOMAIN

AFFECTIVE DOMAIN

WORLD KNOWLEDGE (SCHEMATA)

miscues
sem + sem −

DECODING ACCURACY

DECODING AUTOMATICITY

READING comprehension

ATTENTION

LISTENING COMPREHENSION

RECEPTIVE VOCABULARY

AFFECTIVE DOMAIN

AFFECTIVE DOMAIN

© George J. Cavuto, Ph.D.

Reading Strengths:

Reading Weaknesses:

Primary Causations for Reading Comprehension Difficulty (if present): [w/explanation]

Secondary Causations for Reading Comprehension Difficulty (if present):
[w/explanation]

Primary Causations for Listening Comprehension Difficulty (if present):
[w/explanation]

Secondary Causations for Listening Comprehension Difficulty (if present):
[w/explanation]

CASE 3

Felix is a fifth-grade student. He has been doing poorly in social studies and
English/language arts; he excels in math and science. His teacher and parents are
quite confused as to the reasons for Felix's poor performance. He appears to be
motivated; however, he has performed poorly in the aforementioned areas since
the beginning of the school year. This performance is consistent with his performance since third grade; prior to that, Felix was an "A" student in all areas. His classroom teacher has made the following observations:

*Felix is a mystery to me! He is such a bright young man, first to raise his hand to
answer questions about the meanings of words, current events, science or social studies concepts; however, after he reads the chapter in his social studies text, he has difficulty answering the questions (both factual and between the lines); he has similar
difficulty answering questions after reading literature (both in class and at home). On
the other hand, he is an active participant (i.e., answering questions and participat-
ing in discussions) about the chapter book that I am reading 15 minutes a day to the
class. Felix takes out books from both the classroom library and school library; how-*

ever, he rarely finishes them. He excels in science; we don't use a science textbook—our science curriculum consists of "hands on" science experiments and demonstrations. When called upon to read in class, Felix's oral reading is fast and fluent. He appears to be giving his best effort; however, his grades for this quarter in social studies and English/language arts will be C+ and C respectively. I don't understand what's going on with him—maybe it's a question of maturity!

Felix's parents have made the following observations:

Felix has been going downhill academically since the first quarter of third grade. He spends about two hours in his room doing homework and he still gets poor grades in some of his major subjects. When we peek in his room to ask him how he's doing, we often see him looking at the ceiling with a frustrated look on his face. We know that he doesn't always understand that which he reads, but no one has been able to tell us why. We've tried everything—buying him books from the bookstore and bringing home books from the public library—he seems to get the books, but doesn't read them. We tried reading some of the same books and then discussing them with him; clearly, even the books that he told us that he did read, he hadn't (i.e., he had difficulty discussing even the most obvious aspects of the plot). We are at our wit's end. We have read to Felix every night from when he was two years old until he was in the third grade. We have lots of books in our house, and Felix sees us reading all of the time. We take family trips and discuss current events. Maybe Felix is just a little lazy when it comes to social studies and language arts; we've talked to him about this and he seems to get upset at this suggestion. Hopefully, in time, it will just 'click' for him; we so much want him to enjoy reading, like we do, and to do well in school so that he can go to a good college. He seems like such a bright kid; it's very frustrating for all of us—especially Felix!

Figure 11-3. Simple Reading Assessment Model (S-Ram).

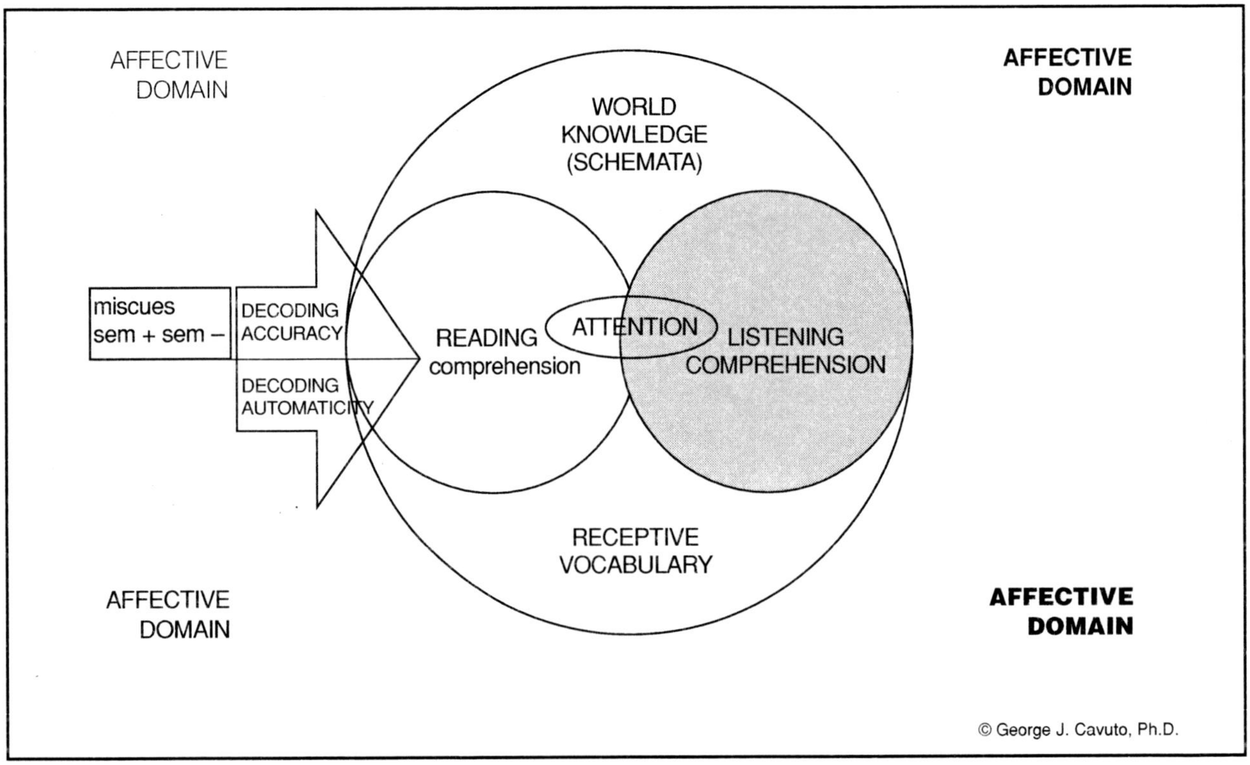

Reading Strengths:

Reading Weaknesses:

Primary Causations for Reading Comprehension Difficulty (if present): [w/expla-nation]

Secondary Causations for Reading Comprehension Difficulty (if present): [w/explanation]

Primary Causations for Listening Comprehension Difficulty (if present): [w/explanation]

Secondary Causations for Listening Comprehension Difficulty (if present): [w/explanation]

CASE 4

David, a fourth-grade student, is having difficulty finishing his seatwork. His classroom teacher has made the following observations:

David has excellent phonics skills—he attacks words very well and is usually successful in correctly decoding words, even those significantly above the 4th-grade reading level; however, he is a very slow reader. His oral reading is slow and plodding; he uses a letter-by-letter word-attack strategy to decode the words that he is unable to recognize at sight; indeed, most of the words in his social studies, science, and language arts texts have to be systematically sounded out. David's oral reading errors often look like the text word but make no sense in the context of the sentence/paragraph. He rarely self-corrects his errors. David has considerable difficulty understanding that which he has read as indicated by his inability to answer written or oral questions (literal and interpretive/inferential) following the reading; however, his ability to remember/understand text that is read to him is excellent. Indeed, his parents tell me that he frequently asks them to read his homework pages in science and social studies to them; usually they refuse, telling him that he has to learn to do his schoolwork himself. David appears to be a very bright child; the school psychologist indicates that his verbal IQ is in the superior range. It often appears that David has difficulty sustaining attention/concentration; however, these difficulties aren't apparent when he's involved in tasks that don't involve reading text (e.g., hands-on science, math calculations). David does very poorly on social studies, science, and language arts tests, usually because he simply doesn't finish all of the questions on the test in the allotted time; the questions he does, in fact, answer are usually correct.

David's most recent standardized test scores are as follows:

Word Identification: 2.5 *(grade level equivalent score);*
                              25th percentile
Vocabulary: 3.0 *(grade level equivalent score)*
                              30th percentile
Reading Comprehension: 2.0 *(grade level equivalent score)*
                              12th percentile

David's parents indicate that he "hates to read and begs us to read his school books to him." Their first response is to refuse to do so; however, they usually capitulate when they see him spending hours trying to do the work by himself. They further indicate that he refuses to take out books from the library that are at his grade/age level; instead, he chooses books from the "kiddy section." They feel that David is a bright child who simply needs to be motivated to read. They are hoping that with maturity it will all come together for David.

Figure 11-4. Simple Reading Assessment Model (S-Ram).

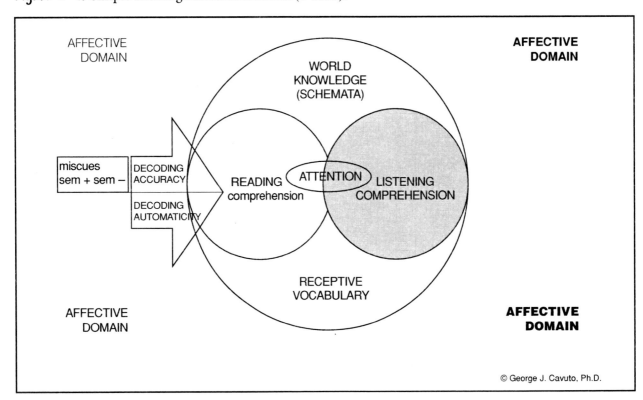

© George J. Cavuto, Ph.D.

Reading Strengths:

Reading Weaknesses:

Primary Causations for Reading Comprehension Difficulty (if present): [w/explanation]

Secondary Causations for Reading Comprehension Difficulty (if present): [w/explanation]

Primary Causations for Listening Comprehension Difficulty (if present): [w/explanation]

Secondary Causations for Listening Comprehension Difficulty (if present): [w/explanation]